D1098047

Tolerance and Compassion

Henrik Wergeland and His Legacy

GYLDENDAL

© Gyldendal Norsk Forlag AS 2008
Published in cooperation with the Norwegian Ministry of Foreign Affairs

Printed in: Slovakia
Printed by: Tlaciarne BB s.r.o., Slovakia 2008
Repro: RenessanseMedia AS, Oslo 2008
Paper: White Offset 120 gsm (1,1)
Typeset: Veronica Sande
Cover design: Egil Haraldsen & Ellen Lindberg | EXIL DESIGN
Picture Editor: Anette Badendyck / Fotoresearch.no
Cover illustration: Carl Peter Lehmann

ISBN 978-82-05-38207-7

Picture Credits

CONTENTS

TOLERANCE AND COMPASSION

In 2008 Norway will be celebrating the 200th anniversary of the birth of one of its greatest poets, Henrik Wergeland. Wergeland was a child of the European Enlightenment and grew up in a time of momentous change for Norway. His reputation as a national poet is due as much to his passionate political and social engagement as to his poetry. All his life he worked tirelessly for religious tolerance, freedom through knowledge and enlightenment, and equality between nations and social classes, guided above all by his profound compassion for humanity.

With his fiery, impetuous temperament and zeal for knowledge, Wergeland would have become deeply engaged in the global challenges we face today. We would have seen him fighting for a more equitable distribution of the world's goods, for nature and the environment, for inter-religious and intercultural understanding; Wergeland regarded religious orthodoxy as an obstacle to political development. He would have continued to champion the cause of freedom of expression and of the press, which he described as "the people's diadem".

We have not yet fulfilled Wergeland's prophesy that "freedom's tricoloured rainbow will fire its rays into the heart of Europe, and one day, *unbroken,* encircle the earth!" If we are going to take the principle that all human beings are of equal worth seriously, we must continue Wergeland's legacy and dare to confront reality. We must refrain from creating enemies out of stereotypes based on lack of knowledge. Wergeland understood this very well. In his own way he fought for the weak and preached tolerance between faiths: "Every religion has a gentle and loving heart," he wrote.

Wergeland's broad involvement in social issues also took the form of practical initiatives that were to have significant effects for years after his death. He believed in humanism as a basis for action. He was a true cosmopolitan in the literal sense of the word, and his most important socio-political work bears the signature "Cosmopolita". We have an obligation to follow up what Wergeland began. We must examine our consciences and intensify our efforts to further the cause of tolerance, cultural equality and respect for human dignity.

The Ministry of Foreign Affairs is contributing to the anniversary celebrations in the form of a project entitled "Tolerance and Compassion". It is addressed to children, young people and adults of all ages and is being carried out in cooperation with the City of Kristiansand, Norwegian Children and Youth Council and the House of Literature in Oslo. This book provides a short presentation of the diversity of the poet's work from a literary and political perspective, and gives a voice to the young people of today through the views of three pupils at the school Wergeland himself attended in Oslo.

We must ask ourselves: Have we become more tolerant? Do we understand each other better? How can we "extend the frontiers of hope", which Wergeland saw as the fundamental condition for human progress?

Oslo, November 2007

JONAS GAHR STØRE
Minister of
Foreign Affairs

ERIK SOLHEIM
Minister of
the Environment and
International Development

GEIR POLLEN

"Hearts of Christians all should glow / With the warmth of Christmas fare"

Introduction to Henrik Wergeland (1808–1845)

Translated from the Norwegian by Alison Arderne Philip

I

The Romantic movement is said to have made dreamers of poets. But of Henrik Wergeland, Norway's greatest poet and the pioneer of modern Norwegian literature, this is at best only half true. His work certainly fits easily into the conventions of Romantic ideology, with its emphasis on the creative subject, and its interpretation of reality as a coherent whole and of history as an organic process of growth, in which the goal is to unite nature and freedom, object and subject. Wergeland himself stressed that he did not read philosophy, or at any rate very little. So was his link with the Romantic movement more a question of character, an innate sensibility, a unique talent? Was it because he had a mind swayed by conflicting emotions, a fiery temperament, a rich imagination, an intense sympathy with the sublimity of nature, a child-like faith, an uncompromising revolt against all oppression, rigid truths, an authoritarian, life-denying attitude to art and to life itself?

The reader need not spend many hours in Wergeland's company before encountering these characteristics in lavish profusion. Wergeland's work is conspicuous for its lack of artistic moderation. The poet's imagination knows no limits, whether he is plunging into the darkest depths of the soul or soaring above the stars, both are invested with the same passion. Occasionally a cosmic *angst* is revealed in a line of poetry, only to be banished by the confidence that only the Poet can feel: he stands between earth and heaven and has seen in every living thing, even the plainest weed, the reflection of a divine presence. This certainty is expressed in the last lines of one of his best known poems, "To a Pine Tree":

> The house of God is Nature's shrine;
> No moss so small, no weed so plain,
> But builds a chapel there.

Wergeland's work is an excellent example of what Friedrich Schlegel, the most important ideologist of the German Romantic movement, called "progressive universal poetry": a new form of poetry that would unite "all the different poetic genres and moods, merge poetry, philosophy and rhetoric, and eliminate the border between life and poetry". This poetic utopia was unified by a completely new belief in the artist as an intuitive creative force: writing poetry stems more from nature than from art. As a natural force the poet is above the conventions of time and place. True poetry, in the sense of progressive and universal poetry can only be realised in total freedom.

For Wergeland, as for so many Romantics, freedom was a religious creed. He worshipped the blue flower of poetry more ardently than grey reality but at the same time he extolled the French Revolution's ideals of liberty, equality and fraternity as part of God's plan for the universe. When, at home in Christiania [as Oslo was then called], he read the newspaper accounts of the revolution that was sweeping the streets of Paris in July 1830, he was fired with zeal. And when king and bishops took harsh action against the people, Wergeland's protests could not have been louder if it had been he himself who was being persecuted.

Like the other Romantics, Wergeland found the world of the 18th-century pioneers of the Enlightenment, with their faith in hard work, the bourgeois virtues, cool reason and sober moderation, too small and too narrow. He rejected a philosophy that viewed society in terms of commerce; nature in terms of eternal, unchangeable laws; objects in terms of immediate, concrete, finite sense perceptions. Wergeland was a Romantic by nature and by inclination; he always wanted to go further, plunge deeper, reach higher.

And yet for all his passionate endeavours to break down doors, push creative boundaries, grasp the world in its universal wholeness, from a grain of sand to the outermost star, Wergeland was also a realist. He used his common sense and had both feet planted firmly in the here and now, in other words Norway and the world at large as they actually were in the years 1808 to 1845, and not as he would have wanted them to be. Wergeland's work has few traces of the yearning tones of other Romantic poets or their fascination with the primeval forest and other inaccessible regions; there is little sighing or mysticism. He had no time for those melancholy, inept young dandies, with their dreamy, languid gaze, who populate the works of so many of his contemporaries. The Romantic longing to reconcile the life of the mind with the life of nature had no place in Wergeland's work; for him this was an outdated idea, a false dichotomy.

In short, Wergeland was a dreamer who did not lose himself in his dreams. He was too much of a rationalist, too much of an extrovert and man of action. Throughout his life he worked for the enlightenment of the common people, the farmers and workers, and his educational texts covered a wide range of subjects, from the cultivation of potatoes to the political situation in Russian-occupied Poland. He wrote an endless number of such booklets, textbooks for schoolchildren from poor families and a book on the history of the Norwegian Constitution; he taught confirmation classes and established public libraries. He was engaged passionately, but with a noticeable absence of diplomatic talent, in political and social issues.

Everything Wergeland wrote had its origins in his own experience. His view of the world is reflected in his ability to amplify, to perceive the great in the small, and this led inevitably to idealisation. His poetry is expansive in every sense of the word. The individual mirrors the universal, the local mirrors the global. To him Skreikampen, a steep stony fell close to his home that is not high enough to feature on any map except a local one, is a point from which to view the whole earth. An ordinary adolescent infatuation is the expression of God's universal love. A friend he admires is portrayed in a poem as a person of extraordinary significance, even genius. Those with whom he happens to be quarrelling or having a legal dispute, who call for an unreasonable expenditure of time and money, are "enemies of humanity".

In the same way his few major journeys, to England and France in 1831 and to western Norway in 1832, were transformed into literature that, though imbued with local detail, far transcended the actuality. The same applies to his many poems that were inspired by daily contact with plants and animals, domestic and wild, which were objects of his passionate love and interest from earliest childhood. His meeting with Amalie Sofie Bekkevold, whom he married in April 1839, resulted in a series of love poems that vibrate with the tension between the deeply personal and the suprapersonal, or universal. The list of great and small issues in which he was fiercely engaged, whether it was Norway's position in the union with Sweden, the struggle for freedom and independence of other peoples and nations, or the medicinal properties of plants, is endless.

The major part of Wergeland's literary production, which included poems, plays, fairytales, essays, stories, letters and articles, was written during a period of 16 years, but it fills 23 large volumes. He wrote for as long as he had breath in his body. His work has a breadth and artistic productivity fully equal to the greatest of European writers of the Romantic Age. It encompasses the story of a writer's life that had no parallel in Norwegian literature, of a nation state in the process of being born, and of the political struggles of many of the peoples in and outside Europe during the first half of the 19th century.

II

Henrik Arnold Wergeland, to give him his full name, was born in Kristiansand on 17 June 1808, the eldest of five children: three boys and two girls. His father, Nicolai Wergeland, was a schoolteacher and from 1812 an assistant pastor. In 1807 he had married Alette Thaulow, daughter of the city registrar in Kristiansand. Nicolai Wergeland was born in Osterøy in Nord Hordaland, but the name is thought to come from Verkland farm, at Brekke in Sogn. The fact that his family name was linked with that of a Norwegian farm [and was thus an unequivocally Norwegian name] was a significant detail in an age when fierce struggles were being fought over the definition of the terms "Norway" and "Norwegian". Henrik Wergeland was proud of his background, and did not hesitate to remind other people of it whenever he felt it would serve his purpose.

In 1817 the family moved to Eidsvoll, where Nicolai Wergeland had been appointed pastor. Eidsvoll is a small town about 60 kilometres north of Oslo. It lies just below the southern tip of Lake Mjøsa, Norway's largest lake, which extends 100 kilometres northwards until it meets the valley of Gudbrandsdalen, which according to tradition was the childhood home of Ibsen's Peer Gynt. The lake is bordered by some of Norway's richest farmland, a fertile, undulating cultural landscape with fields of corn and vegetables interspersed with small areas of mixed woodland. On the west side lie the irregular forested slopes of Totenåsen, with Skreikampen fell, rising 700 metres from the waters of the lake and visible from Eidsvoll. The melancholy "Skreya", as Wergeland called it, is recognisable from his description, but otherwise has few points of resemblance with the craggy Alpine landscape he often evokes in his many references to it:

> Skreya, abode of the clear summer sun with the open,
> red-gold cloudy portal, Where storming snow, as a
> whinnying foal, and mist's chariot
> Rests at night, to foam over Mjøsa at dawn...

Thus Wergeland grew up surrounded by the landscape of Lake Mjøsa – "Norway's heart" as he called it. His father was one of the few state officials in the area. Otherwise, apart from some wealthy landowners, the inhabitants were poor: small farmers, tenant farmers, servants and casual workers. In other words, it was a Norway in miniature. At the beginning of the 19th century 80 to 90 per cent of the population were involved in some form of agriculture and still practised a non-monetary economy. The Industrial Revolution had not yet reached Norway.

The parsonage where the Wergeland family lived no longer exists; it burned down in 1877. Although the surrounding landscape is now criss-crossed by roads, bridges, a railway and housing developments, these have not obscured the views of Lake Mjøsa and Skreikampen, or the rivers Vorma and Andelv, where the young Henrik would have bathed and fished. It was a place he was to love all his life, and he would have had no difficulty in recognising it today.

A whole national mythology has grown up around Henrik Wergeland's boyhood at Eidsvoll, which has been faithfully handed down from one generation to another by teachers of Norwegian. Here he learned to know the country and its people, here he began his "spiritual communication with nature, mixed with the local people much more than was usual among the educated classes, associated freely with eccentrics and other strange characters, did what he could to help the needy", as the researcher Edvard Beyer relates. His bedroom resembled a "natural history museum, a hermit's cave or a magician's laboratory," wrote his sister Camilla many years later in her reminiscences of her brother. "Birds flew about freely. Fish and live grass snakes in glass cages, Bella on a cushion with a gilded collar ... not to mention his favourite, the old rabbit, which ... hopped about among moss, stones and fresh leafy branches." Camilla Wergeland, later Collett, also became a celebrated author, and wrote Norway's first modern novel, *Amtmandens Døtre* ["The District Governor's Daughters"]. Although it was published as early as 1855, it deals with the position of women in marriage and in the family.

This was not the first time Nicolai Wergeland had come to Eidsvoll. He had been there three years earlier, on the occasion of what must have been the high point of his public life and a recurring topic of conversation in the family home for as long as Henrik lived there. For Nicolai was one of the 112 men who assembled in 1814 in the imposing main building at the Eidsvold Verk ironworks, only a stone's throw from the parsonage, for the purpose of drawing up a new Norwegian constitution. Nicolai Wergeland was part of the 15-man committee appointed by the constituent assembly to draft the constitution, and is credited with finding the name for the first national assembly, which met in October: the Storting.

The historic meeting at Eidsvoll was preceded by a series of momentous and dramatic events the like of which nations seldom experience. in October 1813 the coalition between Austria, Britain, Prussia, Russia and a number of German states inflicted a decisive defeat on Napoleon at the Battle of Leipzig. On 31 March 1814 the forces of Alexander I of Russia and Fredrik William of Prussia marched into Paris, and the following week Napoleon was forced to abdicate. The Norwegian historian Knut Mykland has written: "The Battle of Leipzig delivered the final blow to Napoleon's hegemony in Europe. The fate of the double monarchy of Denmark–Norway was sealed on the field of Leipzig." For Denmark–Norway, which had signed a new treaty with Napoleon the previous year, the alliance with France was already over. At 3 o'clock in the morning on 15 January 1814, a peace treaty between Sweden and Denmark was signed at Kiel, under which Frederik VI of Denmark renounced the Norwegian throne on behalf of himself and his descendants. Thus the 434-year-long union between Norway and Denmark – what Ibsen called Norway's 400-year-long night – was over, and Carl XIII Johan of Sweden's plan to rule Norway was crowned with success. In accordance with the Treaty of Kiel, Norway would be "with full Ownership and Sovereignty passed to His Majesty The King of Sweden and constitute a Kingdom united with the Kingdom of Sweden."

However, eight months previously, in May 1813, Crown Prince Christian Frederik of Denmark had been made Vice-Regent of Norway and commander-in-chief of the Norwegian armed forces. Christian Frederik refused to recognise the Treaty of Kiel and put himself at the head of a national resistance movement. His intention was to take the Norwegian throne himself on the strength of his position as heir to the Danish throne. Norway was to be an absolute monarchy, and his long-term goal was to revive the Danish–Norwegian union. On 16 February he convened 21 men "of the highest rank" – officials, landowners and merchants – at Eidsvoll in order to acquaint them with this plan. He was now forced to realise that he had omitted to take one important factor into account: the Norwegian people themselves. The majority of the assembled notables strongly advised him not to have himself proclaimed an absolute monarch; they pointed out that the rights renounced by King Frederik VI had passed, not to him, but to the Norwegian people. Christian Frederik therefore agreed to convene a national assembly to draw up a free constitution, with himself as elected king. As every Norwegian schoolchild knows, this plan was carried out, and on 17 May 1814 the 112 Men of Eidsvoll – 59 officials, 37 landowners and 16 merchants – signed the Norwegian Constitution, and Christian Frederik was elected king the same day.

However, the new king's rule proved to be short. For Norwegian independence to become a reality, one or more of the major powers that had defeated Napoleon would have had to violate the terms of the Treaty of Kiel, under which Norway was Sweden's reward for supporting the allies during the Napoleonic Wars. Christian Frederik had hoped for Britain's support but this was not forthcoming, and faced with the threat of all-out war between Sweden and Norway, he renounced the throne. On 4 November 1814 King Carl XIII Johan of Sweden was elected king of Norway. On his death in 1818, the crown passed to his

heir, the French-born Jean-Baptiste Bernadotte. Bernadotte, who had been one of Napoleon's marshals, had been elected heir to the Swedish throne by the Swedish national assembly in 1810, and thereafter adopted by the childless Carl XIII Johan. On his coronation he took the name of Carl XIV Johan.

This was the historical and political backdrop to Henrik Wergeland's life and work. Later historians incline more and more to the view that the events at Eidsvoll in the spring of 1814 were the last move in a game of chess, in which the pieces were controlled by the major powers and not Norway. Wergeland, on the other hand, was certain in his own mind that the Constitution was the fruit of the Norwegian people's own desire for freedom. According to him this desire had lain buried like a seed in Norwegian soil from the time of the sagas, through the 400-year-long night, until – following the adoption of the American Constitution in 1787 and the French Constitution in 1791 – the plant thrust its way through the earth with an irresistible force. He christened Eidsvoll "the Bethlehem of Freedom" – Wergeland was never afraid of extravagant metaphors. But this was one he sincerely believed in.

Human freedom occupied a central place in Wergeland's cosmology: freedom "comes from Heaven"; it is part of the Creation. The fact that his boyhood home was next door to "the Bethlehem of Freedom", and that his father had participated in the birth of the new, free, Norway, was to him of crucial significance. All his ideas about human freedom, all his actions to promote human rights, sprang from the events at Eidsvoll in May 1814, when Norway fulfilled its destiny. His view of this, to him, historic event on a global scale is expressed in the incomplete *History of the Norwegian Constitution,* on which he worked from 1841 until his death in 1843. He already takes flight in the introductory sentence: "To be or not to be was also the question facing Norway in 1814. Its position was that of a Hamlet between the nations [of Europe] and, like Hamlet, it was heir to a throne, unhappy, betrayed by false friends, and branded as mad by the world." Norway as both the birthplace of Christ and a character from Shakespeare, no less!

III

Thus the title of the poem that opens the eight-volume popular edition of Wergeland's writings, published in 1958, could have been none other than "Norges Frihed" [Norway's Freedom]: "O nations, hear the Word / That echoes from the lowlands of Colombia to the mountains of Norway!"

The poem was written in 1825, the year he took his final examinations at the Cathedral School and began his studies in theology at Norway's first university, which had been established in Christiania only 14 years previously. He had already had a number of literary pieces published in the newspapers. The first of these, the saga of "Blodstenen" [The Bloodstone], appeared in the newspaper *Morgenbladet* on 17 July 1821, and showed no sign that the writer would become a great poet. It begins: "Filled with fear, the wanderer began his descent into the valley of Pöllnitzer-Dalen." There he meets "screeching owls, which build their nests in the fallen ruins of the Chemnitzer fortress". In other words, it was a good example of an infantile Gothic romance. A few years later he was also writing comedies that were performed at the parsonage when he was home on holiday.

During his years at university he published a number of poems and plays, but his real debut came in 1829, with a collection of poems entitled *Poems. The First Ring*. From the first two lines of the opening poem, "To Stella", Wergeland's voice is unmistakable: with its exalted tone, both self-aware and self-assured, the poem seems to draw a deep breath before beginning: "Hah! How wide the span of my soul / Up to Heaven, down to Hell!" Wergeland's imagery creates a universe that expands continually in every direction, often within one and the same sentence. A sensory impression, usually originating in something concrete and perfectly ordinary, triggers a poetic chain reaction where one association sparks off another, image gives birth to image, until the poem reaches its climax in a completely different sphere from where it began. The link with the point of departure is there, but the reader has to strain himself almost to breaking point in order to find it.

For example, in "The Little Rabbit" Wergeland describes Blaamin, his pet rabbit, which hops about on the floor, as "one-eared, three-legged, violet-blue and charming" and immediately his imagination leaps from the innocent down-to-earth world of the nursery rhyme "up to the Heavens", where the rabbit has "a friend", who is the poet's Muse. The rest of the poem is a 10-page Romantic, visionary, pre-Darwinist cosmogony that encompasses the entire Creation, from the humble nettle in the ditch to the outermost stars.

As a true Romantic, Wergeland was making the point that all nature, from the smallest rabbit to the greatest poet, is imbued with the same divine presence, has its origin in "the same sun". He declares that if he were to discover in the rabbit's eye a desire to change places with him, so that poet became rabbit and rabbit poet – "you gain a harp, I gain grass" – he would consider that he had the best of the bargain! Because in the rabbit's "clear eye" he sees "Heaven's wide span". Wergeland shared this perception of the divine unity of the world with a whole generation of Romantics, but what is unique about the poem is the duality in every stanza. Near and far, the tiny detail and the supreme whole, become one. His gaze encompasses both the rabbit in his room, "creeping on the ground", and "the imagination of

the Creator", which only the inspired poet, the Seer, can perceive. These two extremes are also linked in the most natural way by the diction, which alternates elegantly between the comic naivety of a children's rhyme and the visionary language of the Romantic poem.

No Norwegian writer had ever written like this. However, the impulse that prompted this first collection of poems could not have been less original: a young man's normal, stormy, hopeless passion. Wergeland underwent a succession of amorous turmoils in his youth. The objects of his adoration were, in no special order, Ida Haffner, Emilie Selmer, Elise Wolff and Hulda Malthe, and there is every indication that these episodes were a trial for both the young admirer and the young woman caught in his ardent gaze.

Hulda Malthe, the daughter of an official in Romerrike, was two years younger than Wergeland and died unmarried in 1892. She is said to have driven Wergeland to greater depths of despair and lifted him to higher peaks of happiness than any of his other loves. The rich flora of anecdotes that has grown up around Wergeland's name tells how Hulda's refusal drove him to jump in despair off the high ramp leading up to the barn on the parsonage farm, and how, inspired by his hero Lord Byron, he even contemplated running away to Greece to fight – and preferably die – in the Greek War of Independence.

Fortunately for posterity, he chose instead to resurrect Hulda and his hopeless love as a myth in the form of the idealised Stella, the star, who is the leading figure in this first collection of poems. As so often in the course of his life, writing a poem gave him the confidence and strength to conquer the defeat of the moment:

Listen! My Stella! My soul,
Who in harmony rocks
In a cherub-filled heaven.

From the heights of heaven, far from the barn ramp at
Eidsvoll, in the radiance of Dante's Beatrice and Petrarch's
Laura, the ignominious rejection lost its sting. He will meet
his love again, after death, in a heavenly eternity:

The long-awaited day, beyond the passing years,
When my soul meets with yours,
Stella! Stella!

Then they will experience "the joy and peace of a wedding, /
Here in the grove of the blessed", as promised at the end of
this volume. This is a love that is not only as pure as the air
of the Norwegian countryside but that *is* pure air, cleansed of
all the physical, erotic desire that, according to Wergeland,
makes kissing a woman like "eating a ham". Like the star
she represents, the heavenly Stella is the focus of all light
in these poems. She radiates with equal intensity at the
beginning and the end of *First Ring*. Wergeland has filled
the space between these poles, as if to give her shade, with
poems praising his older writer colleague Maurits Hansen,
a selection of friends, the Norwegian flag, King Carl Johan,
Napoleon and the sacredness of freedom, all portrayed in
dramatic images and exuberant language.

Wergeland would probably have agreed with those
authors who claim that rereading their first work is a doubt-

ful pleasure. As a mature writer he regarded these 28 poems as the sins of youth, marred by immaturity, hyperbole and uncertain form. It was not often that Wergeland presented himself in a less than favourable light, but for once it seems that he undervalued these first poems. In terms of form Wergeland is Wergeland from the first line, even though he does not always manage to hit the right note on his first attempt to play, not the lyre, but the harp – the most popular metaphor for poetry used by contemporary writers. The most astonishing thing about this first volume is how it not only anticipates, but also introduces, all the major themes of his writing in subsequent years. The collection could equally well have been called "The Major Theme", since in Wergeland's world great and small are always two aspects of the same whole: nature and art, the local and the global, past and present, eternity and the moment, earth and heaven – everything, including human freedom, originates and is given meaning by the same "imagination of the Creator". The poet's mission is to illuminate this truth for humanity.

IV

This theme is already fully developed in his second work, which could equally well have been entitled "Human Freedom". The first time he mentions the great work that was to follow up his first collection, which he originally intended to call "Heaven and Earth", is in a letter to Hulda's mother, dated 2 April 1828. He says he does not want to write any more comedies, not "allow such unripe fruits to fall from my tree, where a great golden apple is ripening". In a later letter to Hulda he again talks about the poem, and says he is working on a theme "so vast that even Milton's work will seem simple". His plan is to "sing Hulda's praises". When the great golden apple is ripe, the work finished, he will mount his horse, ride to the Malthes' farm, and read it aloud to his future wife and mother-in-law in the garden pavilion "between tea and supper". With hindsight we can say that he would have had to read extremely fast, since the completed poem filled no less than 720 printed pages. Literary historians have called it the most courageous and ambitious poetic work in Nordic literature. By this time it was no longer entitled "Heaven and Earth", but *Creation, Man and Messiah*.

However, some time before the ink had dried on the last verse, Hulda alias Stella had become history. The next object of Wergeland's love was Elise Wolff, five years his senior and "beautiful, rich, independent and learned" – she is said to have spoken seven languages. On 12 September 1828, in a seemingly endless letter asking her to marry him, Wergeland sets out in extraordinarily pedantic and long-winded terms to tell her "the story of my soul", probably, he no doubt felt, making a virtue of necessity, since he had already behaved foolishly and "indelicately", as he expressed it, in proposing so many times to one girl after another. He opens his soul to "resolve his inner disharmony" and in order that Elise may "learn to know me completely". In the letter he is both taking stock of and defending himself: "all my absurdities ... inconsistencies and excesses" are revealed, but also "the good traits in my character". He describes himself as: "of a sanguine temperament, good-natured, passionate, robust, enthusiastic, sensual while having the most ethereal principles and feelings, credulous, enquiring, tolerant ... not egoistic, a good friend, a quick-tempered but immediately repentant enemy, soft-hearted and a friend in deed to the unfortunate ... a lover of people and animals, flowers, in short, of all living things". He assures Elise in elaborate detail that his love for Hulda was merely a brief incident, that even when he was praising Hulda to the skies Elise was his true love. No other love than "the only, the highest, the deepest" love for her, Elise Wolff, has mastered his soul, enthuses the poet, with an emphasis on *no other.* Wisely, Elise thanked him for his proposal but answered it with a friendly but decided no. This time, however, there were no leaps from the ramp in Eidsvoll.

More interesting than these youthfully charming, but overwrought and self-centred effusions, are the passages in the letter dealing with "Heaven and Hell". He compares his stupendous plan for the poem to a Milky Way that fills his soul. Now it is no longer Hulda but Elise who is the "divinity in this poem, where the history of the world, in all its dramatic progress, whose core is the struggle for freedom of ideas and peoples, is merely the backdrop." Wergeland explains that he wishes to reveal a spiritual world, "a poem encompassing the whole world, of which the centre is Stella's life and progress towards perfection, depicted with a brush dipped in the sun. As a measure of time, the history of the world accompanies it in the form of a drama."

If this declaration of the content of *Creation, Man and Messiah* seems confusing to the reader, the poem itself is no easier to make sense of. At first Wergeland seems to have

planned to write a kind of love poem in the Platonic tradition. And what a love poem – to and about the immaterial Stella, who represented the idealised spirit of Hulda or Elise as appropriate. However, when the poem was published, in July 1830, Stella turned out not to be the hub of the universe after all. It is true that the seed of *Creation, Man and Messiah* was sown in *First Ring* and the bitter-sweet experience reflected in those poems, but the love that illuminates the later poem is not for a particular, idealised woman but for all mankind. What at first was described as the back-drop, "the struggle for freedom of ideas and peoples", has become the play itself. Thus Wergeland dedicates the poem to the defenders of truth, freedom and love, together with "my beloved father", Nicolai.

As the title indicates, this far-reaching poem is divided into three parts, each of which describes in wildly imaginative terms a stage in the history of mankind. From the beginning, when the earth lies "cloud-wrapped, steaming, barren" via the earthly life of Adam and Eve, to the end, when the Messiah, the great redeemer, takes centre stage and, in tune with the heavenly spirits, "blesses the brothers of earth, for Earth and Heaven have become one, a choir that praises the glory of God."

Only the first, shortest and artistically the most successful part, "Creation", is included in the eight-volume edition of Wergeland's work. Above the steaming, newly created earth, before the creation of Adam and Eve, hover the two heavenly spirits Phun-Abiriel and Ohebiel. The first is a brooder, beset with nagging doubts: "Is God then in this lump?" The other is filled with love and trust, replying without hesitation to Phun-Abiriel's question "Which sun brought me forth?", "Supreme Goodness". Later Cajahel and Obaddon, spirits of light and darkness, life and death, rise up from the earth. They are opposites, but also conditional on each other: "O without death it is not possible to conceive of life on earth," cries Cajahel in a loving response to "My Obaddon".

The astute reader will already have guessed that these heavenly and earthly spirits, Phun-Abiriel and Ohebiel, Cajahel and Obaddon, are expressions of the forces that are constantly at work in each of us and in mankind's collective history. The conflict between light and dark, life and death, earthly and heavenly, gives us the impetus to move forward, achieve ever higher forms of life, ever greater perfection. Despite their profusion, the tangled branches of *Creation, Man and Messiah* all grow from the same trunk: an indestructible faith in man's capacity to develop himself, a belief in progress. A divine spark is to be found in even the most wretched of lives. Redress will be made. In Wergeland's imagination "the rapid wriggling of the snake" becomes "an angel's struggle to spread his wings" and "Each shall become a Christ, a true son of God".

In *Creation, Man and Messiah* Wergeland draws on ideas from a number of sources that were of general interest at the time, especially among the Romantics. The Bible was naturally the most important of these, but various versions of Platonism and Neo-Platonism, and contemporary publications on for example history, church history and mythology, were also popular. These are interwoven with contemporary politics and Wergeland's own experiences. The autobiographical ties with Stella have already been mentioned. The background for his portrayal of kings and clergy as enemies of humanity was the political situation in Europe after the defeat of Napoleon, when the Holy Alliance between Alexander I of Russia, Francis I of Austria, and Fredrik William III of Prussia, backed by the power of the Church, took action against the revolutionary groups in Europe. Wergeland frequently expressed his deep abhorrence of this alliance.

Many of the most important poets of the time, including Goethe and Novalis, dreamt of writing the great poem that would embrace the entire cosmos, but had found the project too unmanageable. As Ibsen's Peer Gynt says: "To think it, wish it, even want it – but do it! No...". But the 20-year-old Wergeland did do it. A poem like *Creation, Man and Messiah* could never be successful in the sense of being lucid, stringent or harmonious, but Wergeland always considered it his greatest poem. Wergeland's first biographer, Hartvig Lassen, commented that "yet under piles of tastelessness [it] hid his best and greatest thoughts". The first part, "Creation", where the newly created earth still "sighs / In the gentle lap of the sun as if it were a bride" is the best; there is poetry in every line, in the smallest detail and the widest panorama. In the other two parts, which are longer, the fearless 20-year-old gets into more trouble. A prominent figure in literary research, Fredrik Paasche, described "Man" and "Messiah" as having "repetitions and contradictions, an overabundance of rhymes, leaden rhythms, linguistic monstrosities, completely unmanageable tangles of sentences". Every reader who has grappled with the poem will be grateful to Professor Paasche for this clear statement that he too found parts of it to be an impenetrable linguistic wilderness.

V

In spite of its obvious weaknesses, however, the work was not an artistic monstrosity. It could be called the child of a young man's imaginative genius, and it could have remained precisely that: the greatest feat of imagination in

Wergeland's work and in Nordic, and possibly European, literature. But no sooner had the poem been presented to a public that, with few exceptions, understood very little of it, than its author began transforming into prosaic reality the dream called up by his poetic fever, a dream to which he was totally committed: that of an enlightened, free human community. The order of the adjectives is not random; he believed that people must be educated before they can be free.

Wergeland had completed his theological studies in spring 1829, but could not hope to receive a benefice at once. He was not qualified; the minimum age was 25 and a degree in practical theology was required. He therefore returned home and completed his great work. He also began on his work of public education, which would have secured him a place in Norwegian history even if he had not written a single line of poetry. For one who sincerely believed that "freedom comes from Heaven", the ministry and the education of the people were two sides of the same vocation. For Wergeland the pastor and the educator were one. This belief was in the best tradition of the Enlightenment, and Nicolai Wergeland is likely to have emphasised this aspect of his calling when discussing his son's choice of occupation with him. Growing up in those surroundings, Henrik would also have known something of the ignorance prevailing among the working classes. The challenge lay right outside the parsonage windows.

And Wergeland took it on. By the autumn of 1829 he had established a parish society and a public library. He set out his policy platform in the first two booklets of *For Almuen* [For the common people], which were published in the spring and autumn of 1830. The first of these encouraged "the common people to ensure their own education, in particular by reading good literature". The second encouraged them "to form parish societies affiliated with Det Kongelige Selskap for Norges Vel [a society for the development of local communities, now the Royal Norwegian Society for Development]".

Both these educational booklets, which exude enthusiasm and enterprise, were published by the Society. This organisation was founded in 1809 on the wave of patriotism that was rolling over the country, and its mission was to promote literacy and economic development. During the first years of its existence its activities covered a wide field. It published school textbooks and supported the publication of writings by the old Norse authors, when Norway was a great power. It provided loans for clearing new farmland and industrial development, and awarded scholarships and prizes for treatises on subjects of general interest, such as that written by Nicolai Wergeland in 1811 and entitled *Mnemosyne,* which sets out the reasons why Norway should have its own university. The Society also awarded a prize to Henrik Anker Bjerregård for composing Norway's first national anthem, *Sons of Norway.* Wergeland's idea was that the Society should have local branches in the form of parish societies all over the country that would further this valuable work by promoting the economic and cultural development of local communities.

Wergeland realised how important it was to assure the Norwegian farmer that being educated would not keep him away from his daily work by making him "amass theoretical knowledge" all the time. He emphasised that it was the farmer's leisure hours that were to be occupied. "You shall drive your plough with pride; you shall walk behind it as an enlightened, free man, not as an empty-headed slave of darkness who knows nothing more than how to scatter oats in a furrow and then harrow them." Subjects who obediently followed the crowd could never make good use of the freedom Norway had gained in 1814: "You shall learn to prove for yourself what the pastor preaches from the pulpit, judge for yourselves what the judge rules from his seat!"

The following year, in April 1831, Wergeland published a long article entitled "Why does humanity progress so slowly?", in which he points out the link between a national constitution, religion and public education. The main idea is that civil law and religious teaching must match. If one is liberal the other must be so as well. This is because they both stem from the same source: "the continual, gradual development of reason". The reason why humanity had not made more progress, even in states with liberal constitutions, is that the Church and the clergy have kept the people in submission by preaching a religious mysticism that goes against all reason. According to Wergeland the source of the stagnation is to be found beneath the altar. Mysticism must be eradicated, he says, and replaced by a universal humane religion based on "morality and education". The clergy, he emphasises, must renounce their detached role as prophets halfway between heaven and earth, and begin educating the common people. If young people are given an education it will not be long before they learnt to see "the true heaven in ... flowers and, supported only by a blade of grass, follow the path of empiricism to the highest truths." By this means they will be able to develop the power of reason, and humanity will be saved. Only then can the 19th century complete the Enlightenment project, to use a modern term, begun in the previous century. This is Wergeland's conclusion, and it shows that the article is really only a strongly concentrated prose version of the ideas set out in *Creation, Man and Messiah*.

Wergeland wasted no time in composing further booklets. The third dealt with "Useful knowledge for the farmer on the healing, colouring, tanning and poisonous properties of the various plants growing on his land". This was a natural choice, since in addition to history Wergeland was passionately interested in botany, and his poems are full of plant names; they read like the most enchanting verbal herbaria. The fourth booklet was a collection of texts for youthful readers, and contained information on the stars, the earth and the various types of rock. He also distributed long lists of books he considered suitable for public education. They featured literature and manuals on everything from horse-breeding to watch-making, morality to gardening, topography to economics. He also took the time to travel around the surrounding districts promoting the establishment of public libraries. From 1830 to 1837 the number of public libraries rose from 47 to 185. This was not entirely due to Wergeland's efforts but he deserves a good deal of the credit. As far away as northern Norway, a pastor who had been encouraged to establish a parish library reported that the educational booklets had had "an excellent influence" on those farmers who had read them.

VI

However, Wergeland's literary publications during this period could not be said to have had the same "excellent influence". On 15 August 1830, a good month after the publication of *Creation, Man and Messiah,* the newspaper *Morgenbladet* published a poem entitled "To Henrik Wergeland", which opened with the scathing question: "How long will you rage against commonsense, / How long will you wave your quixotic spear?" It went on to pour scorn on the poem, describing it as "an insidious poison", "a fevered nightmare", "a chaos where dragons swim", "fit to frighten the birds", "sheer madness" and "platitudinous", and predicted that the poet would be laughed at and assured a position among the "mad poets on Mount Parnassus". The author of this violent diatribe was none other than Wergeland's colleague, Johan Sebastian Welhaven, the other prominent Norwegian poet of the time. For the rest of his life he was to be Wergeland's bitter enemy.

Welhaven was born in Bergen and, like Wergeland, was the son of a pastor. This, and the fact that they both wrote poetry and were involved in politics, were the only things they had in common; as individuals and as artists they were as different as fire and water, and the conflicts between them are the subject of an entire chapter in Norwegian literary history.

The day after Welhaven's execution by verse, *Morgenbladet* published Wergeland's response. Deeply hurt, but with confidence nonetheless, Wergeland stated briefly that *Creation, Man and Messiah* was being judged by a higher court than that of an anonymous critic. If this higher court were to pass an equally condemnatory judgement on his work, he would lay down his pen, curse the day he had taken it up and declare himself a madman for daring "to compose an epic on the history of mankind, to write the bible of the Republicans". No further defence, he felt, was necessary.

For Norwegians the names Wergeland and Welhaven are inseparably linked, in the same way as Cain and Abel or Jacob and Esau. They give faces to contemporary conflicts that reached far beyond personalities. They stood for opposite poles of the political and cultural struggle for power that was raging in Norway at that time, in which the two sides were as irreconcilable as yes and no, black and white, good and bad. The issues at stake were fundamental: How to build the new Norway? What path should Norway follow in order to discover, or rediscover, its national identity? What did it really mean to be "Norwegian"? There is no doubt about who is the hero and who the villain in the story of Norway's nation-building: Wergeland is the patriot, the genius with the large Norwegian heart, friend of the humble, the children, flowers and animals, the Norwegian flag and the Constitution. The coldly intellectual Welhaven, with his stern, reserved appearance, stood for officialdom, Danishness, in other words un-Norwegianness. These were of course stereotypes at a time when "either/or" had more support than "both/and", and there is little doubt that posterity has been unfair to Welhaven. In a more generous, less bitter and angst-ridden time, the two poets could have joined forces and agreed to disagree. After all, their goal was the same: that Norway should take its place among the free cultural nations of Europe. But they chose instead to conduct a running battle, which must have embittered their lives and taken its toll of energy that could otherwise have been much more fruitfully employed.

The two poets were as unlike each other as two people can be, and this extended to their approach to poetry as well as their politics. As a writer Wergeland was naturally concerned with artistic form, but he had little interest in aesthetics as an academic exercise. His writing was done in the heat of the moment, it was the fruit of a spontaneous subjective impulse rather than of a tradition or a predetermined set of rules. This choice of heated emotions over cool reason is one of the main reasons why Wergeland has been classified as a Romantic poet. Inspiration, that complex concept that many people dismiss as romantic nonsense, appears to have been a real factor in Wergeland's writing. He claimed several times that his poems were created in a state of hypersensitivity combined with a calm "clear-sightedness", in which he was able to transcend distance and simultaneously perceive what was closest and what was furthest away, "as when the loveliest snowflakes lie on the branches and through them one can see infinitely far into the deep-blue air", as he wrote in the autobiographical *Hazelnuts*. Wergeland's description in many ways resembles the lines in an early poem by the Swedish poet Tomas Tranströmer in *17 dikter* [Seventeen poems]: "There is a crossroads in the moment. / [Where] the music of distances comes together. / All grown together in an eternal tree." The final poem is art, but the process of creation, the birth, is nature. Comparing Wergeland's "method" to a volcano, Professor Paasche has written: "Poetry is the eruption of feeling." In his defence of Wergeland against Welhaven's criticism, Nicolai Wergeland compares his son's poetry to birdsong: "I listen with pleasure to the song of the bird, even though I know the bird does not follow notes."

Beauty, for Welhaven, followed its own rules, which were founded on aesthetic traditions and cultural norms, even when the notes were invisible. To him Wergeland's poetry was as raw and unformed as the man himself. Welhaven also talked of "the essence of poetry", and described it as "what cannot be expressed in words"; it is the scent of the word, like the scent ascending from the rosebud as it opens. But he claimed that the scent could only be released through the strict rules of language and the clarity of reason. Poetry is not created in the ecstasy of the moment; it requires the poet to take a step back, reflect, clarify his thoughts, conduct an active dialogue with tradition and aesthetic norms. In the above-mentioned poem in *Morgenbladet* Welhaven says that if the madman Wergeland had known how to preserve the "spark from on high", it would have become "a warm glow". It was this warm glow, as opposed to the devouring fire, that Welhaven cultivated. He has been called the poet of memories, of "emotion recollected in tranquillity", as Wordsworth put it. Welhaven believed that it was only then that soul and language could mirror each other to form a clear, and clarified, image.

Thus Wergeland's and Welhaven's artistic approaches were completely different, and represent two different phases of the Romantic movement. Romanticism in the Nordic countries did not become widespread until the 1830s, and was mainly inspired by the German movement. The great Romantic writers in the Danish-Norwegian tradition were level-headed pillars of society past their first youth, such as Oehlenschläger and Ingemann, both of whom were inspired by medieval Norse literature. The young Wergeland, with his uncompromising subjectivity, his revolt against all political and aesthetic authorities and conventions, and his admiration for Shakespeare and Rousseau, was closer to English giants like Byron and Shelley. In terms of German Romanticism he was closest to the late 18th-century *Sturm und Drang* movement and Jena Romanticism. Welhaven, with his cultivation of tradition, history and national subjects, and his compliance with neoclassical literary norms, was a direct descendant of the later phase of the rather backward-looking Heidelberg Romantic nationalism. This was the conventional Romanticism, reactionary in both form and content, that was in fashion at the time when Wergeland and Welhaven were fighting for hegemony on the small Norwegian Mount Parnassus. This was what Wergeland was rejecting in "To a Young Poet", where he warns the poet against looking backwards to "the rune-covered stones" and "the grave-mound, barbaric days hiding". Instead he should have the vision that leads the way to the future: "The song of the Seer is the herald-hurled lightning."

The two poets also had completely different views on what this future should hold, or more specifically on how Norway was to acquire the national identity they both agreed it needed. Welhaven belonged to the Intelligens-partiet [Intelligence Party], or the "friends of Denmark", as they were often called. The members supported the new Constitution just as strongly as all other good Norwegians, but felt it would be madness to sever the cultural ties with Denmark. In their view the path to cultural fellowship with Europe led through Denmark, especially since this country had a living literary tradition on which Norway had fed all through the centuries of union between the two countries. The class of officials, who were the main culture-bearers in Norway, also possessed most of the political power. These officials had been mainly educated in Denmark; they had friends and acquaintances there and felt at home in Copenhagen. A considerable number had also been born there.

As the son of an Eidsvoll man who in 1816 had written the extremely provocative and one-sided *Sandfærdig Beret-*

ning om Danmarks politiske Forbrydelser imod Kongeriget Norge [A True Account of Denmark's Political Crimes against the Kingdom of Norway], Henrik Wergeland belonged to the Norwegian Party, or Patriots as they were also called. This faction maintained that Norwegians were fully able to do the job themselves. They had a proud Norse past and a culturally uncorrupted class of farmers; this was the earth from which Norwegian culture would blossom. The Patriots were enthusiastic about the increasingly prominent political role the farmers were beginning to play in the 1830s. The future was in the hands of the unspoiled Norwegian people instead of the Danified officials who had been imposed on them during the union with Denmark.

The Intelligence Party in general, and Welhaven in particular, considered the Patriots' promotion of the farming classes and the true Norwegian spirit to be immature boasting, isolationist demagogy, a lot of hot air. Welhaven expressed his opinion on nationalism in *Norges Dæmring* [Norway's New Dawn], a poetic cycle consisting of 76 satirical sonnets that was published in 1834. The main theme of the work is the distaste and discomfort felt by the cultural elite at having to live in a nation whose intellectual life had not yet awakened, where feats of valour were empty words and heads were shrivelled. Although the poem pays a warm tribute to Norway and the Norwegian farmer, the praise is wrapped in a fog of artificial language reminiscent of the sagas, which blurs the outlines of both the country and the farming classes: "O as a blushing, valorous youth, / Shall [the Norwegian] line mature behind the high mountains" and "Farmers! your native soil / Is a sacred land".

In spite of this accolade to national romanticism, Welhaven was making the point that Norwegianness was not something that could be declared; it had to grow over time, in symbiosis with its surroundings. Welhaven's position on the question of nationalism was markedly conservative; he was against sudden changes and believed in tradition and continuity. Although Welhaven was not a reactionary, *Norges Dæmring* caused an uproar, and Nicolai Wergeland responded with: *Forsvar for det norske Folk og udførlig Kritikk over det berygtede Skrift Norges Dæmring* [A Defence of the Norwegian People and an Exhaustive Criticism of the Notorious Publication *Norges Dæmring*], in which he furiously attacked Welhaven. The following, relatively moderate, quotation indicates the level of invective: "It is pure profanity for the Norwegian people to call this ungrateful creature son."

In its views on poetry the Intelligence Party was entirely on the side of Welhaven. And his supporters numbered a good many prominent figures in Norwegian life, like Anton M. Schweigaard, who became the country's leading jurist and was a member of the Storting for many years, Fredrik Stang, who became a member of the government and later prime minister, Professor of History P. A. Munch, and Peter Jonas Collett, Professor of Jurisprudence and a discerning literary critic. Collett later married Wergeland's sister Camilla, who as a young girl had nursed a hopeless love for none other than Welhaven himself. A fact that did not make it any easier to reconcile the two camps.

However, it would be misleading to say that these two groups stood for the establishment versus the underdogs. Wergeland's supporters included men in important positions

such as the historian and politician Ludvig Kristensen Daa
and not least Henrik Heltberg, the legendary gymnasium
teacher who in addition to Ibsen numbered Bjørnstjerne
Bjørnson, Jonas Lie, Aasmund O. Vinje and Arne Garborg
among his pupils – in other words the cream of the generation of writers that followed Wergeland and Welhaven.

The relationship between Wergeland and his father has already been described. It is doubtful whether there are any other cases in world literature of a father and son linked by such a strong bond. Nicolai was Henrik's trusted editor, adviser and friend throughout the latter's turbulent life as a writer. Nicolai was also his son's most frequent and most faithful defender, and shared Henrik's views on all the main artistic and political issues. We know that Nicolai not only made corrections and deletions in his son's texts, he also proposed additions, which Henrik often accepted. As a young man Nicolai had written a couple of novels, and it is likely that he was realising his own ambitions as a writer through his son.

In 1832 Welhaven published *Henrik Wergelands Digtekunst og Polemik ved Aktstykker oplyste* [Henrik Wergeland's Poetic Art and Polemic Propounded], in which he publicly slaughtered his rival. This was too much for Nicolai; the following year he replied with *Retfærdig Bedømmelse af Henrik Wergelands Poesi og Karakteer* [A Just Assessment of Henrik Wergeland's Poetry and Character]. The main point in this defence is reminiscent of the ideas of Novalis, the supreme Romantic and originator of the symbol of the blue flower: "In his own world of ideas, his home, the poet is king," wrote Nicolai. Thirty years earlier Novalis had written: "The criticism of poetry is an absurdity", and in 1829, the same year that Wergeland published his first volume of poetry, Victor Hugo had written, on the subject of neoclassical literary norms, "the vast garden of poetry, where there is no forbidden fruit." By God's mercy the poet is not obliged to follow any beaten track. Genius goes its own way, and the public, as mere mortals, must simply accept this. Welhaven's insistence on the strict rules of language and the clarity of reason is irrelevant.

What makes the conflict between Wergeland and Welhaven so interesting to later generations is that it reflects the intellectual climate of the 1830s in Norway, or more precisely in Christiania – a small town on the periphery of Europe, with a tiny population of 15 000 souls. It must have seemed unbearably cramped to two such large personalities, both of whom were battling fiercely for what they considered to be sacred causes: poetry and the Norwegian nation. Thus writing and nation-building, poetry and polemic, were tangled together in an unhappy mixture. Wergeland and Welhaven personified the two opposing ideals. When their paths crossed in the street – an unavoidable event in such a small town – it must have seemed like a clash between two mutually irreconcilable images of the Norway of the future. Norwegian society was all too easily inflamed; it was not surprising that sparks flew. Established authority was in a state of flux. In the years following 1814 people were satisfied to applaud the principles of the Constitution; in the 1830s they wanted to see these principles put into practice. The farming class was marching into political life and the established officials were afraid of losing power. Norwegian social institutions had only just been born: Norway's only university, temple of the intellect and most prominent symbol of Norway's emergence as a cultural nation, had been established in 1811, and the Bank of Norway and the Stock Exchange, temples of mammon, only later, in 1816 and 1818 respectively.

The enthusiastic Wergeland could now exult over Norway's newly won freedom: "O nations, hear the Word

/ That echoes from the lowlands of Colombia to the mountains of Norway!" He was convinced that "no nation has ever experienced a more wonderful year than Norway did in 1814". But if the nation had been able to see itself in a modern mirror, it would have seen a face whose features were irregular and unfinished. Norway wished to be itself, i.e. Norwegian, but what did it mean to be Norwegian when the country's language – the reflection of the people's soul – was Danish? The most telling illustration of this paradox is that no other generation of Norwegians had written a purer Danish than that used by the Men of Eidsvoll in the Constitution. Much had been won, but much remained to be achieved.

VII

This was the situation when Wergeland, who was not yet 30, began on his great project for the education of the common people, a cause he espoused passionately until his death. In 1836 *For Almuen* was replaced by *For Menigmand,* which in 1839 became *For Arbeidsklassen* [For the Working Class]. He completed the last number in this series in spring 1845, as he was dying. When Wergeland spoke about the importance of education for the nation and the people, his language often soared to heights of rhetoric, but the hyperbole and lofty ideals were founded on a sober realism, and his view that a viable democracy stands or falls with education, with a public who can read and write, and form and give expression to opinions, is still current today.

The parliamentary elections of 1832 resulted in a political landslide: 43 farmers were elected, over twice as many as in the previous elections, and only 33 officials and academics. The balance of power had been rocked. The Intelligence Party lamented the people's "crudeness" and complained that only a few of the new Storting members possessed the knowledge and education required for such high office. They complained, but that was all. Wergeland, although he naturally took the side of "the representatives of crudeness", also realised that they lacked the necessary education to make full use of their new power, and zealously set himself to repair the omission.

Thus the point of departure for Wergeland's education project was the state of the society into which he was born, which stemmed from the events of 1814. However Wergeland extended this perspective to include the world community and humanity in general. The first words of Article 1 of the Universal Declaration of Human Rights, "All human beings are born free and equal in dignity and rights", which was adopted by the United Nations General Assembly in 1948, could have been written by Wergeland himself, with one exception: he would probably have written "created", not "born".

Wergeland continued living with his parents in Eidsvoll until October 1834 when, tired of waiting for a benefice, he moved to Christiania to study medicine. He had passed the examination in practical theology the previous year, but the main reason why he was not given a benefice, in spite of repeated applications, was that he had become involved in a lawsuit that was to dog him for the next 12 years. In *Morgenbladet* in September 1829, with his usual disregard for such petty considerations as proportion and consequences, he had accused a friend of his parents, a certain Procurator Praëm, of being "a traitor to the state and humanity". This was based on Wergeland's opinion that Praëm had been guilty of harsh treatment of the poor. Praëm sued Wergeland for libel, and the latter had to put aside his writing and appear in court.

This apparently trivial case was to follow Wergeland until 1844, when he was ordered to pay costs, which had by this time reached a sum he had absolutely no possibility of raising: 800 *speciedaler* [two *speciedaler* were equal to one *rix-dollar*]. Wergeland's public behaviour was controversial, and his actions put an end to all hope of being granted a benefice by the Church of Norway. However, he did deliver several sermons. One of them, preached in the chapel of Akershus Castle in 1836, had a title that summed up his attitude to his writing: "Seize the essence of things, the meaning of signs, the great in the small!"

In spite of conflicts and worries of all kinds, the 1830s were intensely productive. He made steady progress with his public education project, which he pursued with undiminished fervour. His ability to think in practical as well as idealistic terms is illustrated by the way he collected books for the patients at Rikshospitalet [the national hospital, established in 1826] "for the use of patients who have permission to read", and for the members of the guard at Akershus Castle. Wergeland often came into collision with the military, but he was not a man to hold a grudge. His educational booklets covered a wide range of subjects, from "On Norwegian language reform" to "A speech to humanity on humanity by Vesle-Brunen [the name of his horse]", in which Norway's decidedly most articulate horse calls on humans to treat animals humanely.

The 1830s were a time of political upheaval abroad as well as at home. Wergeland's quarrels paled into insignificance beside the major uprisings in other European countries during this period. Wergeland wrote about them in poem after poem, such as "A Liberated Europe", "Caesaris" and "The Spaniard". All three dealt with the July Revolution in France in 1830 and the fires this ignited in other parts of Europe – Belgium, Poland, the Italian states – which were forcefully put out by the rulers concerned.

Wergeland was particularly moved by the fate of Poland, pulled apart as it was between Russia, Prussia and the Hapsburg Empire; he felt that the same fate could easily have befallen Norway at the end of the Napoleonic Wars. In "Caesaris", which had previously been called "Nicolais" and later "Czaris", Wergeland castigated Nicolas I of Russia for his brutal suppression of the Polish revolt. The Tsar had sent thousands to their death and thousands more to Siberia, closed the University of Warsaw and Russified the school and judicial systems. The poem was written in 1831, directly after these bloody events. It is thought that Nicolai Wergeland persuaded his son to change the title from "Czaris" to "Caesaris" out of a fear of the Norwegian authorities' possible reactions to an attack on the Tsar.

In the opening stanza Wergeland points an accusatory finger at God himself: "God of justice, will you abdicate your throne? / Shall it be mounted by the Caesar of slavery?" and follows it up with descriptions of the Tsar's brutalities that are excessive even for a poet who did not know the meaning of the word moderation. Caesaris – there can be

53

no possible doubt as to who is being referred to – is worse than Satan himself, for he beats nations that are innocent with his "fiery sceptre", while Satan confines himself to punishing sinners. Wergeland calls on Satan to take over Caesaris's earthly throne; the people would greet him with joy if only they could be freed from Caesaris's devilish rule. No wonder that Nicolai was worried about his son's welfare. Apart from anything else, there was the question of the much-desired benefice. The King's approval could be decisive, and Carl Johan, whose explicit political goal was to improve relations with his eastern neighbour, was not likely to overlook the outpourings of a Norwegian poet against the Russian Tsar.

"Caesaris" was published in May 1833. In the dramatic lyric "Spaniolen", which had come out a couple of months previously, the point is the same but the plot is different: a liberal escapes from King Ferdinand's reactionary Spain, and the King pursues him from country to country. Finally he arrives in Norway, "where freedom's heaven shines bright-ly", only to meet his death in the Norwegian mountains. With his dying breath he declares that although countries and men may perish, freedom was born with the first angel, and will not die "until the last soul has died". Not until then will it withdraw its soul and return "to the bosom of God".

The idea for this poem probably came to Wergeland in the summer of 1832, when he travelled on foot through the Gudbrandsdalen valley, over the mountains of Jotunheimen to Bergen and Sogn in the west. The message of the poem is taken from "A Liberated Europe": "For freedom from Heaven comes. / Were the angel[s] not free, there would be rebellion in Heaven." In June 1831 he had made his first and only journey abroad of any length. He had sailed in the *Clara Maria* across the North Sea to England and travelled from there to France. It must have been a great relief to get away from the storm in the local teacup and into a more cosmopolitan atmosphere. This is reflected in the poem that immortalised this journey: "Paa Havet i Storm" [Storm at Sea], where the poet at one moment "flies ... over the tops of the waves", freer than a gull, only to dive in the next instant "deeper than the swan", down to the bottom of the sea, where he hears "the beating heart of the earth". Wergeland is in his element. And what a heady experience for the easily stirred Wergeland to walk the streets through which the revolution had raged only a year ago! He had idolised France since boyhood: home of the Revolution, Napoleon, the tricolore, "Land of all life / Where in the sun of liberty shall grow he whom you baptised Man."

VIII

In this turbulent, blood-spattered period of European history, Wergeland was engaged on many fronts at once. His prodigious output of poems, articles, plays, educational booklets and speeches encompassed not only Norway but the entire world. Most of the shorter poems expressing his patriotic engagement were included in his second collection, *Poems. The Second Ring,* published in 1834. His literary production was already extensive, and even though the works for which he is most famous had yet to be written, and even if he had stopped writing fiction in, say, 1835 and spent the last 10 years of his life writing useful educational material or engaging in politics, his reputation as a great poet would still stand. Many still regard him as the nation's foremost poet, only rivalled by the other great Henrik in Norwegian literature: Ibsen. However little he was known outside Norway, Wergeland would still be classed as one of the great Romantic poets in European literature. This is no small achievement for a man who had not yet reached the age when many Norwegian writers of today are publishing their first volume of poetry.

The most striking quality of Wergeland's poetry is his eye, one could almost say his ear, for the tiny detail that mirrors the greater context, the ability to perceive parallels among a wealth of impressions. He brings together apparently irreconcilable ideas to create a meaningful whole. All an artist's evocative power depends on this ability. In almost all his poems Wergeland uses metaphors and similes that are not to be found in any other Norwegian work, either past or present, and rarely in any other national literature. In this respect Wergeland denies himself nothing. One of the many illustrations of his rich imagery is the first stanza of "Det befriede Europa" [A Liberated Europe]:

From the Caucasus? Gleams my soul from the
Caucasus?
From Skreya-ha? Gleams my soul from Skreya-ha?
Cold, still, glittering on Skreya's summit as a chunk of ice
Lit by the midnight sun,
It looks out over the Earth, while my heart stands still.

Hartvig Lassen, who was an admirer of Wergeland, nevertheless referred to these wonderful lines as "complete foolishness", and meant it in all seriousness. The linking of the
geographical name of Skreya with the interjection "ha!"
to make a brand-new Norwegian word, fully worthy of
the bravest linguistic tightrope-walker, and the image of
the soul as a chunk of ice on the summit of Skreya, lit by
the midnight sun, must have far exceeded the limits of the
acceptable for the able, highly literary and cultivated
intellectual Lassen. Foolishness? Well the imagery certainly
flies in the face of nature: the combination of Skreya, ice
and the midnight sun is a geographical and meteorological
impossibility. One must travel north of the Arctic Circle
between May and August to experience sunshine at night,

and ice can only be found on Skreya in the dead of winter. But should we not be grateful to Wergeland for suspending the rules of geography for the sake of poetry? What grandeur in his foolishness! The unity of the one fiery, icily intense chunk of ice with the cold, majestic panorama in the single moment when the poetic image unfolds: Wergeland's poetic cosmos is mirrored in a single chunk of ice.

At the beginning of 1836, Peter Jonas Collett, lawyer, literary critic, friend of Welhaven and future husband of Camilla Wergeland, wrote a detailed literary assessment of his future brother-in-law in his diary. The knowledgeable, sober-minded Collett criticises Welhaven for being so blinded by his hatred of Wergeland that he fails to see or praise any work of Wergeland's that really does have merit. "For there is plenty left to criticise," he adds. In Collett's strict but just and impartial eyes, Wergeland, with all his faults, is "still a great genius". *Farvel til Stella* is "enchanting"; it is ridiculous to deny that "there are Shakespearean strings to his harp", which will ensure that he will be remembered when many of his descendants are in their graves. For the accomplished man, says Collett, sees gold in Wergeland's poetry where the ignorant man sees only stone. But, he goes on, Wergeland's imagination is at the same time his good fortune and his downfall. It takes him to heaven but also straight to damnation. At his worst he quite uncritically piles image on image, and crams parenthesis into parenthesis even when they are "as appropriate as a fish head in a pearl necklace, or a rose in a chamber pot". According to Collett, what has harmed Wergeland most is that he was published too young, while he was still too immature. He concludes by saying that Wergeland is generally despised, at

least by the leading party, which is the group that surrounds Welhaven.

Collett also gives a lively and as far as one can judge accurate picture of Wergeland the man. He has given up his dissolute lifestyle, Collett tells his diary. He is big and strong, but is thought to be weakened by drunkenness. He then gives a colourful description of Wergeland in a highly emotional state, when the blood flowed to his heart "at such a speed that it must have been positively foaming". Wergeland resembled a volcano that was about to erupt, says Collett, who was present on this occasion. His least flattering comments concern Wergeland's drinking habits; when drunk he could go berserk and pay no heed to anyone, not even his father. Collett records that at a dinner given by Pastor Rynning in Kongsberg his cousin witnessed a scene where Wergeland, after making a circus of himself at the table – knocking over wine bottles, hitting out in all directions – rushed out into the courtyard, ran up a hill, took off all his clothes and rolled in the snow. This is a picture of a young writer with a degree in theology whose behaviour at parties was marked by a complete inability to control his impulses. The wise, sympathetic, but rather naïve Collett was understandably puzzled by Wergeland's character. He ends this diary entry with a resigned sigh: "[his character] is deep, profoundly deep, and my inexperienced eyes are unable to see into it."

If his character was obscure, his gifts as a poet are easy to see. With masterly lyricism his poetry unfolds in a dithyrambic interplay between a white-hot focus and a dizzying bird's-eye view. The eye of the rabbit Blaamin reflects praise for God on high. This is Wergeland's poetic voice: his

register of subjects is extraordinarily rich, but is never far from a song of worship and praise.

In his last love letter to Elise Wolff, Wergeland characterises himself as both "cherub and animal". His behaviour was often so bizarre that this is a fitting description. However, the split does not seem to have had any special influence on his poetry. Behind the storm of images he was basically an idealist, and his inner sense of security is never overwhelmed by irreconcilable forces; his stanzas are not riven by ambivalent emotions. Wergeland the poet was never in doubt about his view of the world: life was good and nature was God. God created the heaven and the earth and made man the steward of His magnificent Creation. Love and reverence for all living things, tolerance and limitless respect for the principle that man is created free and shall live in freedom. These, for Wergeland, were the highest virtues. It is the duty of every Christian soul to work diligently and honestly to bring the world one small step forward along the path to the perfection that Wergeland never doubts exists: it exists because this was God's meaning when He created the world. Everything that stands in the way – especially oppression, lack of freedom, prejudice – is essentially unnatural. His message is hardly new. But it gains a new freshness through Wergeland's amazing ability to express it in images that are used and combined in previously unheard-of ways.

IX

The path from glorification to idealisation is never long, and to judge from his poetry Wergeland must have had an unusually strong need for people he could look up to and idealise. This can be seen in the poems to Stella and in the many poems he wrote to friends and others who shared his views. These were usually patriots in one form or another. His poems are peopled with freedom fighters – writers, politicians, soldiers, from a wide variety of nations. Whether their names are Byron, Delavigne, Washington, Lafayette, Weltzin, Kosciusko, Hooghvoorst, O'Connell, Chlopici or Paez – all of them are the most splendid heroes because they fought, and when necessary died, in the sacred cause of freedom. Among these were Napoleon, that son of the French Revolution, and King Carl Johan. The latter seems an unlikely hero, given Wergeland's often expressed republican sympathies, and I shall return to this question later. Of course the halo of glory Wergeland placed around these heads, especially those of his friends, did not always correspond to the greatness of their thoughts or deeds, but Wergeland's admiration, born of the moment, lifts him so high that his feet leave the ground and he transforms ordinary honest citizens into brilliant geniuses. Nevertheless there is no doubt that his praise was deeply sincere – that he genuinely believed in their genius.

This dithyrambic trait in his personality, if a trait can be dithyrambic, is also evident in his writings about nature and the lives of animals and plants. He was especially interested in botany, but his poems also make frequent references to birds and insects, particularly butterflies. When early one spring morning he invites the butterfly to fly in through the window and settle on his pen, so that the pen may regain its gentleness and his fancies flow through it in "the beauty of thine innocence", this is not merely an expression of empathy with nature, it also shows his awe and worship of "such little ones". Published in the newspaper *Statsborgeren* in the spring of 1837, "The First Butterfly" is one of Wergeland's most beautiful poems.

Wergeland had assumed the editorship of this newspaper, which was an object of abhorrence in conservative circles, two years previously. It was the main voice of the farmers' opposition, and had no hesitation in pillorying officials under their own names when the editor scented an abuse of power. This poured oil on the fires lit by his enemies, which were already burning brightly.

Wergeland was used to having enemies, and was philosophical about it. In "The First Butterfly" he is even grateful to his enemy for his "glance of hate", which provides warmth by kindling the poet's anger. His friend's glance, on the other hand, has often been so lukewarm that he finds more warmth in the eyes of his dog. As I shall show below, several of these friends were soon given an opportunity to become even more lukewarm. But prior to this a new feud broke out between Wergeland and Welhaven and the Intelligence Party. It culminated after Christmas in 1838 in the "battle over *The Campbells*" – a ludicrous episode that occurred at the newly opened Christiania Theatre.

In 1837 Wergeland had written the song drama *Campbellerne eller Den hjemkomne Søn* [The Campbells, or the Returning Son], which was partly based on the work of Robert Burns, some of whose poems Wergeland had translated. Wergeland entered *The Campbells* in a competition for the best Norwegian play, which was held in connection with the opening of the Christiania Theatre. The competition was won, not by Wergeland but by the experienced playwright Andreas Munch; however the theatre bought *The Campbells* as well. On the play's second night Wergeland's enemies in the Intelligence Party attended in force and booed the actors. It was a bizarre sight: Schweigaard, Stang and a number of others who later became leading figures in Norwegian politics hissing and booing until they were blue in the face for the sake of a mere play! To add to the commotion, Wergeland's supporters had also turned out en masse and the resulting mêlée ended with many of the future members of the Storting, ministers, prime ministers and so on being thrown out of the theatre. Wergeland himself had for once been sensible enough to stay away that night.

Wergeland, that "apostle of crudity", as the most influential booers loved to call him, interpreted the episode as a vindication of his talent as an artist, but like his other dramas, the play was not very successful dramatically speaking. The best part is undoubtedly the Prologue, which is entitled "The First Time" and in the true spirit of Romanticism praises the first appearance, the first moment, rather than the final completed work: the courage of the eaglet in the instant when he dares to spread his wings and trust that they will bear him above "the dizzy depths". This, says Wergeland, is the eaglet's real triumph, this is the moment "he first his eagle birthright knew."

As a playwright Wergeland certainly needed to comfort himself with the greatness of the first appearance. Shakespeare was the writer he most admired, and he made many attempts to emulate him in comedies, tragedies and song dramas, most of them involving references to the current political situation. And yet these efforts failed to produce good plays. Why? Perhaps the answer lies in the fact that Wergeland's genius was fired by the mood of the moment, by enthusiasm, sympathy, anger. The patient, meticulous work of developing a dramatic plot that is lucid, convincing and engaging, a well-rounded character who is more than just a two-dimensional type, was something Wergeland never quite managed, however hard he tried. "His real element is the purely lyrical," he wrote in 1844 in a short account of himself in *Læsebok for den norske*

Ungdom [Reader for Norwegian Youth]. This book was written not long before he died, and contains a short presentation of each of the over 100 writers whose works are represented. His assessment of himself is an accurate one: the best parts of his plays are without exception those where he forgets to be a playwright and becomes a poet instead.

In the spring of 1836 Wergeland was given a position at the University Library, which he held until 1840. Although he naturally benefited enormously from the access to books, his ambition was to be a pastor, not a librarian, and he had still not given up hope of a benefice. In 1838 it looked as if he would finally succeed. He had avoided anything resembling a public scandal for so many years that he was promised a position as assistant pastor in Nannestad, only a few kilometres from his beloved Eidsvoll. The pay was poor but Wergeland was enthusiastic. However, this time too his hopes were dashed; the authorities got to hear of a party enlivened by punch and guitar-playing that Wergeland had attended at the home of an officer in the King's Guard, and once again a benefice receded into the distance.

In "Beautiful Clouds" Wergeland makes wonderful poetry out of this rather deplorable incident, using the setting sun as a symbol of the benefice that disappeared. But however beautiful, the poem could not cancel out reality. The foolish punch and guitar-playing episode was all the more unfortunate because he had just become engaged to a girl of humble birth, the 19-year-old Amalie Sofie Bekkevold, and wanted to establish a home. Amalie Sofie lived at the seaward end of Skippergaten, where her father kept a small shop. Today it is the site of Grei Café, which boasts of being Oslo's oldest eating-place. With the money earned from *The*

Campbells Wergeland had bought himself a small house below Ekebergåsen, on the south side of the bay where Oslo's new opera is located. In order to get to the University Library he had to row into town, and had received permission to keep the oars of his boat in Bekkevold's shop. It was here he first met Amalie Sofie, whom he married in Eidsvoll in April 1839. The pair of oars that still hang in Grei Café are said to have belonged to Wergeland.

If the young bride was unable to share her bed with an assistant pastor, she did receive a bouquet of 14 love poems that would have melted the heart of the most demanding of women. The poems were published in the paper *Bien* in August and September 1838, modestly entitled *Poems*. In one of the best known, "The First Embrace", the poet cries: "Come to me, grief, on my bosom press, / Lest it should burst with joy's excess", for it is on his breast that the head of his beloved has lain. There is no doubt that Wergeland was a past master in the art of falling in love. *Poems* also demonstrates that he had become much more skilful in extolling the beloved than he had been in his youthful poems to the incorporeal Stella. Love has been brought down to earth again. The position of assistant pastor had disappeared in "beautiful clouds", but Amalie Sofie is all the more physically present in *Poems*.

It was King Carl Johan himself who had deprived Wergeland of the benefice in Nannestad. He had arrived from Stockholm just before Christmas 1838 to take up residence in Christiania and escape the critical voices of the liberal opposition in Sweden. Carl Johan was popular in Norway at this time because he had acceded to the Norwegian people's wishes on the question of the right of Norwegian ships to fly the Norwegian instead of the Swedish flag when sailing in foreign waters. This issue was of enormous importance for the Norwegians' self-image, and Carl Johan had had the political wisdom to give way, albeit reluctantly. The same applied to the official celebration of the 17th of May [the date of the signing of the Constitution]; the King was not at all in favour of this manifestation of Norwegian wilfulness and independence, but had bowed to "the will of the people". His reward was popularity. On his arrival in Christiania on that December evening of 1838 he was welcomed by a "splendidly illuminated arch of honour" and enthusiastic cheers of "Long live the King!" from the crowds in front of the palace.

Wergeland was also there to cheer the King on that damp and dismal evening, after which he went straight home and wrote a poem in the King's honour, which was printed in *Morgenbladet* in January. Entitled *Kongens Ankomst* [The King's Arrival], it begins with Wergeland comparing his own poetry to "an outlawed harp", from which freedom, love and pain have sounded, and behind whose strings may be glimpsed "the colonnades of the Republic". Having thus dealt with his republican sympathies, the poet goes on to pay tribute to the King. Carl Johan could not have been very worried about this talk of a republic – he was used to it – because he is said to have had the poem translated into French and to have liked it very much. But not so much that he was willing to pay for it with a benefice and ignore the King's Guard episode.

However, the King did offer Wergeland an annual pension of 200 speciedaler from the privy purse. The pension was to be granted for two years, after which the King promised to reconsider the question of a benefice. Wergeland accepted the offer, but stipulated that the money should be regarded as payment for his work in the cause of public education. Thus he was able to use the pension to publish *For Arbeidsklassen,* a paper that contained much useful information and also dealt with cultural matters. The paper's largest print run was 4000, and the articles fill 700 pages of Wergeland's collected works.

It did not take long for Wergeland's enemies to sharpen their knives. Scathing attacks appeared in both *Morgenbladet* and *Den Constitutionelle:* how could he, a sworn champion of liberty, a declared republican, who had called his major work, *Creation, Man and Messiah,* "the Republicans' bible", accept food from the King's hand? Wergeland defended himself by emphasising that the money was payment for work performed, but the words stung. Worst of all, the knives were being wielded by some of the closest friends of his youth, led by the historian and later Storting member Ludvig Kristensen Daa. "Parted Friends", which Wergeland addressed to Kristensen Daa in 1842, is an expression of the pain he felt at this treatment; the last two lines read: "O had my memories faded, / Had thine less swiftly gone!" He signed the poem *Der Geächtete,* "the Outlaw", a signature he was to use several times in the succeeding years.

X

Wergeland's admiration of Carl Johan is an interesting paradox in his personality. The most uncompromising rebel in contemporary literature and politics, who flouted every rule of behaviour when it suited him, was devoted all his life to two father figures, his real father, Nicolai Wergeland, and Carl Johan, with his French roots. "I loved him with a child's fresh love," Wergeland confided in *Hazelnuts*. He often drove his father mad, and Carl Johan to fury, by his intemperate behaviour, but he never doubted that the King had a fatherly sympathy for him even when he behaved in such a way that "made it impossible for [the King] to show him any mercy."

One of the reasons why Wergeland invested Carl Johan with a golden halo was that he was born in Wergeland's beloved France and rose to prominence during the French Revolution. In Wergeland's eyes, he had also ensured Norway's freedom in the drama following the events of 1814. This is not the place for a discussion of whether this view of Carl Johan's political role in Norwegian history is justified. Wergeland was no political analyst. It was Carl Johan the man, and what Wergeland perceived as his humanity and generosity, who evoked the poet's love.

In an article Wergeland translated from the English, the difference between prose and poetry was explained as follows.[1] The first deals with the naked reality of things; the second populates the elements with "fantastic forms and attributes to the earth a heroic spirit, a reason and a beauty that do not belong to it." Wergeland's acceptance of these definitions says more about him than the definitions do about prose and poetry. Again we see the irresistible need to

---

[1] *Translator's note:* the quotation is not from the original article but is a direct translation of the Norwegian.

admire, to idealise, to laud to the skies. A dithyrambic poet needs a king.

In 1840 Carl Johan extended Wergeland's pension for two more years and increased it to 300 speciedaler a year. Not content with that, and against all recommendations, the King appointed Wergeland Director General of the National Archives. But both these unequivocal gestures were taken by Wergeland's critics as proof that they had been right all along: Wergeland was a traitor who had sold his soul to Carl Johan. The suspicion cast on himself and his motives in almost every quarter made the start of the 1840s perhaps the hardest period of Wergeland's life. Even when the fighting between the patriots and the Danophiles had been at its fiercest, it had never been difficult for Wergeland to get his views printed in the national papers, but now all his contributions were refused, and he was forced to turn to the provincial papers.

The criticism and calumny must have hurt him deeply, and given him the feeling that not only the cultural elite, with whom he was used to quarrelling, but also the people themselves, had turned against him. How else to explain that, in the teeth of the storm that was raging round him, he turned to Johan Ludvig Heiberg, the leading Danish critic and Welhaven's mentor in matters aesthetic, and asked him to use his influence to get his, Wergeland's, work published in Denmark? Despite his "uncompromising nationalism," wrote Wergeland, he would rather "belong to any other great literature than the Norwegian." Wergeland had previously had little time for this writer of vaudevilles and arbiter of aesthetic taste, who was admired in Christiania as well as in Denmark and who had dismissed *Creation,*

Man and Messiah as "a poem as thick as the Bible and more difficult to understand than the Bible's most difficult book."

But in spite of his enemies' vicious accusations, Wergeland had not altered his political stance. He himself considered that with age and maturity his writing had become "less vehement than before, just as in certain matters I have adopted less emphatic views." Posterity has often called Wergeland a revolutionary, but this is at best an imprecise description, for his political engagement was always, even in his tempestuous youth, driven by a kind of radical compassion with its roots in his interpretation of Christianity, and not by any political ideology or materialistic analysis of power relations in Norwegian society. He believed that the common people's path to power led through enlightenment, knowledge, education, not through class conflict. Just as he could sing the King's praises without being a royalist, so he could laud the revolution without being a revolutionary – Wergeland could never be accused of compromising. Unlike Karl Marx, whose *Communist Manifesto* came out only three years after Wergeland's death, Henrik advocated, not the people's right to take power, but the duty of the powerful to share it with the people.

In 1840, in the midst of his difficulties, Wergeland composed *Jan van Huysum's Flower-Piece,* which is not only his most romantic poem, but also one of the most beautiful. It is about loss and grief, but also the redeeming power of art. It is not impossible that he chose this particular subject at this particular time as a way of consoling himself. The poem was inspired by a painting by the Dutch painter of still-lifes Jan van Huysum, and on this Wergeland builds a fantasy, partly in verse, partly in prose poetry, about a pastor called Adrian who loses his entire family in a fire. Old and half-mad from grief, Adrian lives like a hermit in the ruins of his burnt-out church. His only consolation is the flowers he sows among the ashes and tends with loving hands; in them he sees his wife and children restored to life. One day a stranger – Jan van Huysum – walks past and is struck by the beauty of the flowers. He immediately wants to paint them, and although the old man begs him not to, he cuts himself a bouquet. Because "There is no more violent, ruthless, selfish passion than that of the painter. It knows no limits, no right or wrong. It seizes the object of its desire with the arms of a giant, because it believes it has the heart of a god."

Robbed of his flowers, Adrian dies. But Jan van Huysum takes the bouquet home, places it in a vase and paints the same picture of it year after year, driven by his gnawing conscience, "an overwrought, unbalanced anxiety", in a never-ending search for perfection. But the day comes when his soul is forced to admit that the picture is perfect. In that instant a drop of water falls from "the crystal-clear air" onto the painting, where it breaks into a shower of droplets that stick to the flowers and cannot be removed. Jan van Huysum realises that these are Adrian's tears falling from heaven and cries exultantly: "Old man! You are redeemed." From that moment the painter's heart is once more at rest. More romantic sentiments could hardly be imagined.

The book came out in July 1840 with the following dedication: "A bouquet from Henrik Wergeland to [the Swedish writer] Fredrika Bremer". On 6 August Wergeland wrote a letter to Fredrika, excusing himself for not having written to her before and explaining why: every poor man or woman in Christiania who wants to write a begging letter, every widow needing advice and comfort, comes to him for help. "They stand at the door of the pavilion [in the garden, where he used to write], just when I believe myself to be alone; [not even] a cat could walk more softly, and a poem or a good intention is ruined."

Towards the end of the letter Wergeland sums up the political situation in Norway, and indirectly his own political position, by saying that the union enjoys broad support among Norwegians. Furthermore, the people agree that they must educate themselves in order to "prepare political reforms and strengthen freedom". In the Storting "the people's demand for education measures becomes increasingly audible and more readily acknowledged", and he adds that the new municipal organisation has greatly contributed to this tendency. He was referring to an act that had been passed in 1836 by the Storting, where the farmers continued to be heavily represented, giving the municipalities greater autonomy. In other words the causes dear to Wergeland's heart – public education and more democratic government – were receiving wide support. The political upheavals resulting from the July Revolution, whose echoes had even reached as far as Norway, had calmed down, and relations between the King and the Storting, the farmers and the officials, had become more peaceful than they had been in the 1830s. Wergeland no longer needed to fight constant battles in the newspapers, and could concentrate on other forms of writing.

XI

In Wergeland's best play, the tragedy *Barnemordersken* [The Child Murderess], written in 1835, the following line is spoken by Mairen i Carpentras, one of the play's disagreeable characters: "a Jew can be compared to a forbidden book." This rather mysterious simile is one of the first statements made by Wergeland on a subject that was to occupy him more than any other during the last years of his life: the position of the Jews in Norway. As early as 1687 Christian V had passed a law prohibiting Jews from entering Norway without a royal letter of safe conduct. Most recently the last sentence in Article 2 of the Constitution, which Nicolai Wergeland had helped to draft, read: "Jews are still not permitted to enter the Kingdom."

For Henrik Wergeland this passage was a stain on a constitution that he otherwise praised as the freest in the world and an example to all peoples who were fighting for justice and freedom. In two articles in *Statsborgeren* in March and April 1837 he claimed that Article 2 contradicted the genuinely liberal spirit that imbued the other provisions of the Constitution. He pointed out that citizens of states that "are otherwise groaning under the most indubitable despotism" have greater freedom of religion than Norwegians, and that this is in harsh contrast to the enlightened freedom otherwise evident in Norway's constitution. In his view Article 2 should only contain a provision establishing general freedom of religion. To do his father justice, it is worth noting that, although Nicolai Wergeland had not only approved but even advocated excluding Jews from the Kingdom, he gradually came to share his son's views.

Wergeland's argument for amending the wording of Article 2, popularly known as "the Jewish provision", was primarily a question of principle. It has already been mentioned that he regarded freedom as "coming from Heaven". In a more earthly vein, he claimed that freedom of religion was a fundamental freedom, on the same level as freedom of speech, freedom of association and freedom to conduct commercial activities without interference by the authorities. Article 2 was in conflict with elementary Christian duty and ordinary compassion. But just as he did in his other efforts to educate the public, he combined high ideals with a down-to-earth utilitarian approach. By opening up the country to the practitioners of other religions, he pointed out, the authorities could replace some of the losses caused by the growing emigration to America. As a patriot, Wergeland had a low opinion of those who were abandoning their mother country instead of helping to build it. He never knew that by the end of the century over half a million Norwegians would have crossed the Atlantic in search of land and fortune in the new world, which meant that only Ireland of all the European countries would lose a higher proportion of its inhabitants to America. So Wergeland emphasised the Jews' well-known capacity for hard work and their long experience of the manufacturing industries. These were the workers the Fatherland needed! "They would soon make use of the waterfalls with which nature has endowed us to set up factories, and enliven our rivers with steamships," he wrote. In other words, he was advocating what we now call socially beneficial labour immigration. Underlining the usefulness of repealing the Jewish provision was of course also a tactical measure intended to appeal to business interests in the Storting.

In June 1839 Wergeland submitted the following proposal to the Storting: "That the last sentence in Article 2 of the Constitution, which reads: 'Jews are still not permitted to enter the Kingdom' is deleted." The proposal was accompanied by an 18-page document setting out his reasons. While his strong engagement shines through the text, his arguments are supported by facts and presented in the level-headed prose of a civil servant. There is no trace of the rhetorical tone of his earlier treatises. Wergeland cites state after state in Europe and shows how they give their citizens greater religious freedom than Norway does. Norwegian religious intolerance is only equalled by that of Catholic Spain, says Wergeland. He examines and refutes Norwegian prejudices one by one: that the Jews are not ready for civil emancipation, that their character as a race is depraved, that they would withhold money from the state, that they would arrive in such hordes that they would take over all commercial activity and in this field outnumber the original population – prejudices that can be heard to this very day in debates on immigration. Wergeland states that it is a historical fact that countries that have opened their borders to Jews have had no reason to regret their liberal policy; on the contrary, they have benefited from their just actions. Norway lacks people and money, Wergeland reminds the members, nor is the spirit of enterprise of its inhabitants very developed. This is where the Jewish people would be able to make a substantial contribution, for "this ill-treated people possess a morality, a spirit of enterprise and a stamina that others would envy them."

The President of the Storting, S. A. W. Sørensen, liberal Supreme Court advocate and member for Christiania, had already, in 1833, put forward a proposal for "freedom to practise their religion for all Christian religious sects", which did not, however, get as far as a debate in the Storting. He now adopted Wergeland's proposal as his own, and it was decided that the matter would be debated during the next parliamentary period, which would begin in 1842. In the meantime Wergeland continued to collect evidence in support of his cause, and conducted an extensive correspondence with Jews in Sweden, Germany and other countries. However, in a letter dated 9 September 1842 to Michael Simon Warberg, a businessman in Gothenburg, Wergeland describes how the proposal had been rejected that day by 51 votes to 43, after a debate lasting seven hours. Wergeland had watched the debate from the gallery, and tells Warberg how President Sørensen was repeatedly overcome by tears as he listened to the speeches.

An amendment to the Constitution required a two-thirds majority, and Wergeland had not counted on achieving this at once. Although he was deeply disappointed that the great majority of farmers, who were to be the backbone of the Norway of the future, voted against, while the officials and urban representatives voted in favour of the proposal, he was on the whole satisfied with the support the amendment had received, and believed it would lead to victory at the next attempt. In a treatise entitled *Jødesagen i det norske Storthing* [The Matter of the Jews in the Norwegian Storting], written a couple of months later, he summed up his view as follows: "time will not allow lead weights to stop it in its flight." This was in the true spirit of the Enlightenment, whose proponents had an unshakeable belief that truth and reason would always ultimately prevail over bigotry. Wergeland's thinking was in line with that of the great 18th-century Enlightenment pioneers – Voltaire, Rousseau, Diderot, Locke, Hume, Lessing, Kant. There would be setbacks, and the proposal would continue to be greeted with contempt, especially when expressed in verse, but the poet must not lose courage, he must never give up. Wergeland says in the "The Army of Truth", the prologue to the poetic cycle entitled *The Jew*:

> Onward yet, brave words, undaunted
> Though so few!
> Earthly triumph has to you
> By the God of light been granted,
> Who are serving
> Truth, his child, with faith unswerving.

This small volume, which makes no bones about its message, was published in 1842 and subtitled *Ni blomstrende Torneqviste* [Nine Blossoming Briar Shoots]. The dedication opens with the words: "These words from the heart are dedicated to the Norwegian Storting." Wergeland intended to convince the members by a combination of documentation expressed in prose and sensitivity expressed in verse, appealing to them to right the wrong done to this people in the Constitution.

Even as early as in his first published volume of poetry, *Poems. First Ring,* Wergeland had expressed the hope that "May Christian, Muslim, Heathen, Jew / Ultimately meet each other / In their common Father's arms". But nowhere else in his work are tolerance and compassion, the cornerstone of Wergeland's engagement in freedom of religion, better expressed than in the poem "The Three", the second and in this context undoubtedly the most important text in *The Jew*. It begins with a prose passage praising the hospitality of the East: "What beautiful temples of human love are the public inns of the Orientals!" In such an inn, "chance brought together a Mohammedan, a Christian and a Jew." "After friendly converse" the travellers fall asleep to the soft lullaby of a spring emerging from the earth under the plane tree among whose roots they lie. Morning comes, and a mist covers the desert. With the first rays of the sun, "Each of them wished to greet God in his own way", but because of the respect for each other they have developed during their talk the previous evening, they remain silent, "afraid of hurting the feelings of the other two." This embarrassed silence is broken by a bullfinch, a wagtail and a thrush, who settle on the same branch of the tree and begin to sing in chorus. The travellers take this as "a sign from heaven that our praise too will be pleasing to the Lord, although we express it differently." The mullah sings, "Allah! Allah, great and good!" the rabbi, "Now all glory to Jehovah!" and the monk, "Praise be to Almighty God!" They then shake hands and set out joyfully along their various routes: the mullah to Baghdad, the rabbi to Damascus and the monk to Jerusalem.

"Every religion has a mild and loving heart" is written in italics in "The Three". For Wergeland this was a self-evident and fundamental truth, but one that his fellow Christians sinned against only too often. The heart-breaking

81

ballad "Christmas Eve" recounts the story of how one Christmas Eve the Jewish pedlar Old Jacob is struggling through a snow storm on his way from Sweden to Norway, when suddenly he hears a child crying. He finds a little girl, half dead with cold. He presses her to his breast and continues stumbling through the forest until he finds a cottage. But the couple who live there refuse to open the door when they hear who it is; they would let "the dog, but no Jew enter a Christian house!" The following morning they find Old Jacob and the child outside in the snow, frozen to death. With horror they discover it is their own child, their little Margrethe. She had been in care at a neighbouring farm, and had wanted to spend Christmas with her mother and father. "Oh, God has punished us! / Not the fierce storm but our own cruelty has killed our child!"

Although it seems petty, not to say sacrilegious, to criticise such genuine engagement and sympathy, *The Jew*, with its overly didactic tone and almost childlike enthusiasm for the cause, is more of a moving – and hard-hitting – document of its time than great literature. "The Army of Truth", which has occupied a permanent place in Norwegian textbooks for generations, is the best poem in the book. "The Jewess" is also a great poem; it is inspired by Wergeland's fascination with the strange and exotic, although it takes very much the ordinary man's view of women: "Put off your veil O Jewess, put it off, Rachel, thou wondrous beauty!"

In a new letter to Warberg dated 22 July 1844, Wergeland tells him about his plans for a sequel to *The Jew* in the same vein. *The Jewess. Eleven Blossoming Briar Shoots* was published in October. Wergeland called it a twin and sequel to *The Jew*, and like *The Jew* it is poetry written for a particular purpose, to plead a cause, with Jewesses as the heroines. Below the title is written the word *charis*, Greek for "favour, grace", and in poem after poem Wergeland praises the noble character of Jewish women; they are compassionate, tolerant, faithful and responsible. The Christian Church, on the other hand, is slated in such scathing terms that no one would think the poem was written by a Protestant theologian. In the final poem, "Etterretningen" [The Message], the "tower of the Christian Church" is "hard and proud"; it has "a spire whose weathervane tears the bleeding clouds". The poet expresses his sympathy for the crows that circle round the tower, unable to find a place to perch and rest. "For the tower is without mercy, like the Christians' Christianity." In a preceding poem "A Voice in the Wilderness", he says that "Hearts of Christians all should glow / With the warmth of Christmas fare, / Honey-sweet, / Heaped for all the world to eat", but instead they are ice, lumps of snow and stones.

Like its predecessor, *The Jewess* is not one of Wergeland's finest works. It contains too many poems that are primarily didactic, filled with a burning zeal but two-dimensional and stereotyped in terms of both characters and conflicts. However, among these chiefly narrative poems there are a few that stand out from the rest and have a quite different, bolder and more personal, tone. It is as if Wergeland realised that an extra pair of wings was needed to lift a collection of poems that, while they arouse our sympathy, are rather ordinary compared with his best work. One of the best is "Follow the Call!", which, like "The Army of Truth" with which it has several themes in common, is a classic example of Wergeland's art.

Wergeland begins many of his more philosophical poems, which deal with freedom, justice and enlightenment, and the role of poetry and the poet, in a mood of discouragement, but soon he rises to a triumphal faith in his own strength and that of the common people. In "Follow the Call!" the poet is a "Royal eagle, captive made, / Broken-winged with fettered limb," which has been forced to serve as a humble watchdog "by a lonely cottage door". He has had the misfortune to be "of a little nation born, / In a spot remote, forlorn, / With a speech / Which can never further reach / Than the uttered breath may go." But then the mood changes: "Young as yet the world must be". Are we not still undeveloped, still only a cradle-song, a tale that has only just begun? We still have a long way to go before the seeds sown in us by the Creator can grow to maturity. So, Wergeland admonishes the poet, stop complaining! Stand up and fight " as if God's own voice invest / With a storm thy heaving breast". Few, "just a little band of friends", will hear your words, but that is enough. Look at nature, where nothing, however tiny or unimportant, is wasted, and all decay serves a purpose. Every summer the moss "tiny silver cups will shed / On the grey and barren crag." A thousand years later "lofty pines" will grow there, in the earth created by the decayed moss.

XII

"Follow the Call!" is full of vitality and optimism, as essentially Wergeland as it is possible to be; it is both a programme of enlightenment and a statement of belief. It would have made an excellent prologue to *The Jewess* instead of "On the Sickbed". In this latter, deeply personal poem, with its almost raw sensitivity, Wergeland interweaves the Jewish cause with his own life and death. Many changes had taken place in Wergeland's life since the publication of *The Jew* in the spring of 1842. The two older colleagues he most respected, Maurits Hansen and Anker Bjerregaard, had died within a short time of each other that spring. Wergeland wrote a memorial poem to each of them. The most quoted is the poem he wrote for Bjerregaard's funeral. When in the second verse he writes that life's pain will be redeemed on the other side of the grave, and that the judgement of the world will now transform "thrown stones to golden fruits", there can be little doubt that he was thinking of himself as much as of the dead writer.

A more devastating loss was that of Alette Wergeland, "the most tender of mothers". She died unexpectedly in August 1843, while Henrik and his wife were visiting her at Eidsvoll. Wergeland wrote one of his most personal and moving poems in her memory, in which he comforts himself with the thought that he will consecrate a room in his house to her, which will be called the "Blue Room". There will always be fresh flowers on the table; her spectacles, the book she never finished, her knitting, "at which she was a true expert" and her footstool will all be there. One day he will lay *The Jewess* on the table. It will appeal to her, he says, since the love he so often saw shining in her gentle eyes embraced not only the family but also "strangers and the poor".

On 8 March 1844 King Carl Johan died, at the age of 81, at the Royal Palace in Stockholm, and on 26 April he was buried. The King had attentively followed Wergeland throughout the ups and downs of his career. Wergeland had written a number of poems praising the King as a benefactor of the people and had accepted money from him. Even at the cost of friends and public esteem, his devotion had been unshakable. In the last poem he wrote to Carl Johan, "On the Funeral Day of King Carl Johan", he comforts himself with the thought that there will be: "a flower to deck my robe of mourning – / That I have loved my king the most."

A week later, on 2 May, Wergeland himself had to take to his bed; a cold had developed into pneumonia, which in the end was to cost him his life. In a letter to Warburg he blamed the damp walls of Akershus Castle, where his office was located. At the beginning of May it had been unusually hot, and Wergeland had not wanted the stove in his office to be lit. One morning he arrived in his office covered in sweat, threw off his coat and began working only in his shirtsleeves, without noticing that the room was freezing cold. It was not until an hour had passed and he felt icy shivers running down his spine that he realised how cold he was. He felt so ill he had to go home and go to bed, and "I've been lying here ever since the 2nd of May," he wrote.

In "On the Sick Bed", Wergeland provides a poetic report on his state of health in August 1844: what is the significance of "These stabs of flame, this icy thrill / Which shivers through my breast?" he wonders anxiously, but soon he is full of defiance and energy, in the true Wergeland spirit. Let death believe it has won a victory. For the poet the pains in his breast are: "the wayward airs of Spring stirring in

Heaven ... the blessed April of my salvation!" The poem continues to fluctuate between resignation and defiance of "invading Death". At one moment the poet is mourning the loneliness imposed on him by his enemies, those "raging fools", the next he claims that this same loneliness is prouder and fairer even than "Brazil's inviolate forest". Because, he says, "Here too of visions there is no lack", and he is visited by "spirit forms". Not until the last verse does he find rest. He feels that his mother has come to him in the shape of an angel and lightly laid a finger on his brow. His soul is a "dew-washed flower ... / New-born in innocence." All the conflicts, between life and death, friend and foe, are resolved: "I have forgiven all!"

The letter to Warburg in July is an unembroidered, unsentimental account of his illness in prose. He tells Warburg how he has managed to smuggle in a book about lung diseases, from which he gathers that his symptoms are dangerous: "a collapse of the surface of the lung, so that the cells disappear and the lungs are filled with phlegm". He then gives a short, concise outline of his literary plans, the first of which is to complete *The Jewess*. "Should I die," he adds, "my sincere and heartfelt efforts on behalf of Israel's people will mean that my last thoughts will be happy ones." The poem and the letter in their different ways sum up his situation as it would continue to be until his death the following year: on the one hand a disease that was slowly but surely, day by day, cell by cell, destroying his body; on the other hand, despite being wracked by fever and fits of coughing, an indefatigable literary output.

From his sick-bed the dying Wergeland wrote a number of poems and prose pieces, which he put togeth-

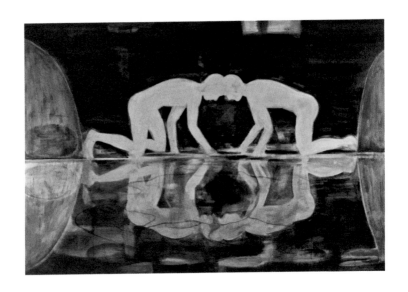

er in the autobiographical *Hazelnuts*. These are among his best works. He completed the lyrical epic *The English Pilot*, which is mainly based on his visit to England and France 13 years previously. He continued to produce *For Arbeidsklassen* and edited the young people's reader *Læsebog for den norske Ungdom*. He continued to correspond extensively. He revised *Creation, Man and Messiah*, which he still considered his principal work, and produced a more easily accessible but also more insipid version, which was now called simply *Man*. His last work, written when he was markedly weaker, was the ballad opera *Fjeldstuen*. The artistic fruit of the most famous deathbed in Norwegian literature was nothing short of miraculous, both in terms of quantity and, with a few exceptions, of quality.

In addition to this prodigious output, he had to devote time to visitors. These included a number of his previous adversaries, who, now that this insufferable writer and henchman of the King was on the brink of the grave, had decided to make their peace with him. One of these was Ludvig Kristensen Daa, the friend of Wergeland's youth who had given him the most painful stabs when the latter had accepted financial support from Carl Johan. In a letter to Daa two months before he died, Wergeland was able once more to call him "my good friend". The letter was addressed to Daa in his capacity as member of the Storting and drew his attention to a situation Wergeland had himself experienced when admitted to Rikshospitalet with a very painful earache. He complained that the long corridors gave a frightful echo that filled the building. This made it unusable for "pathological and surgical patients", who needed rest, and he recommended that a new hospital should be built for these patients. He proposed that the members of the Storting should themselves pay a visit to the hospital and "investigate the matter".

In the midst of all this Wergeland received the bill for the 12 years in which the absurd and unfortunate Präem case had been making its way through the courts. He was being required to pay costs, which had amounted to about 800 speciedaler. This was a complete impossibility for Wergeland; his finances were already in a poor state, and would now be precarious. In order to ensure an income for his wife Amalie Sofie after his death, he decided at the beginning of 1845 to sell Grotten, the house the couple had built a few years previously in the south-west corner of what is today the park of the Royal Palace. As a substitute he was permitted to build a simple cabin, which he immediately christened "Welcome", in the neighbouring street of Pilestrædet. He was carried here in a closed, but draughty, litter on 15 April. Wergeland immortalised this heartrending episode in "The Grotto at Auction", which has been a fixed part of the Norwegian curriculum for generations of schoolchildren, who have waxed indignant over the evil-minded lawyers who could so cruelly plague a dying man. But the man, at any rate if he is called Henrik Wergeland, does not give up, for "Yet one thing in my breast is left / Beyond the clutch of law" – his genius.

Of all that Wergeland managed to produce during the year he was confined to bed by illness, the handful of poems he wrote after he moved out of Grotten, from 20 April to 20 May, are those that have been most widely read and appreciated by posterity. For the average Norwegian poetry reader these six poems *are* Henrik Wergeland. Three of them, "At Night in Hospital", "Second Night in Hospital" and "A Possible Confusion", were written during his few days at Rikshospitalet, where the doctors had sent him so that he would not be exposed to the damp of the unfinished Welcome or disturbed by the hammering of the carpenters. The verse form in these three poems is the four-line ballad stanza employed by Heine, in which only the second and fourth lines rhyme. In spite of his lack of familiarity with it, Wergeland mastered it easily and used it as effortlessly as Heine does. The stanzas follow each other in an elegant rhythm, like the tail of a cat as it saunters across the floor, alternating between irrepressible humour and extreme gravity. They are a marvellous example of Romantic irony. The poet is lying awake in the large hospital; he feels that the full moon shining through the window alleviates his suffering. But the moon is bringing not alleviation but death. The roses it casts through the window and scatters over the bed and the floor are not blood-red, like the roses whose praises he has sung so often, but faint and white: "When you are as white as my roses, / Your pain will rest at last."

"O Spring! Spring! Save me! / No one has loved thee more dearly than I", prays Wergeland a month later in "To Spring". In one of his many letters to his father, dated "20th May 45, 7 o'clock in the morning", he describes this poem as "probably my last poem, perhaps the most sensitive". The unrhymed, free-flowing lines are addressed directly to nature – the blue anemone, the dandelion, the coltsfoot, the swallow, the gnarled old tree, which he has loved more than any earthly riches because they are "Spring's daughter", "Spring's children", "Spring's messenger". Now he calls on them to witness, to kneel and pray that Spring, their lord, will save him. Surely the old tree, "venerable as a patriarch", will be heeded when he stretches his arms towards heaven and "[cries] out for me, although he is hoarse." On Norway's national day, 17th May – the last he was to experience – he wrote to Nicolai: "I die a deist, a sincere devotee of Allah; out of respect I do not take it upon myself to imagine the details of what awaits me in the next world". He found such beauty in this world, in the wallflower and his canary, that his imagination could not "picture anything more beautiful".

However, despite his prediction, "To Spring" was not his last poem after all. When it was published in *Morgenbladet* on 24 May, it was accompanied by "The Beautiful Family" and, not least, "The Wallflower", perhaps his most beautiful and best crafted poem. This alone would have assured him a place among the greatest of poets. No longer can the spring flowers, the maple and the swallow pray for his life. Calmly he asserts that he will never see the wallflower in his window fade and die or the rose bloom:

Wallflower mine, ere thy bright hue fades,
I shall be that whereof all is made;
Ere thou has shattered thy crown of gold,
I shall be mould.

When 'Open the window!' I call from my bed,
My last look lights on thy golden head;
My soul will kiss it, as over thee
It flieth free.

Twice do I kiss thy lips so sweet,
Thine is the first, as it is meet;
The second, dearest, remember goes
To my fair rose,

whose flowering blooms I shall never see;
So give it my greeting, when that shall be,
And say I wished on my grave would all
Its petals fall.

Yes, say I wished that upon my breast
The rose thou gavest my kiss shall rest;
And, Wallflower, be in Death's dark porch
Its bridal torch!

XIII

And finally, what happened to the last great political cause that Wergeland worked for, and continued working for until his death: the question of allowing Jews to enter the Kingdom? In "On his Sick-bed" he himself had predicted that he might not see all eleven briar shoots blossom, in other words the repeal of the provision banning Jews, in his lifetime. His prediction turned out to be accurate. The amendment was debated in the Storting in 1845 and 1848 and defeated both times. It was not until 1851, six years after Wergeland's death, that the Storting finally passed an act repealing the provision.

Wergeland died on the night of 11 July 1845, only 37 years old. He was buried in the cemetery of Vår Frelser's Gravlund, which contains the graves of many of the most prominent figures in Norwegian history. The funeral was attended by "a crowd more numerous that has ever been seen before in Christiania", wrote Hartvig Lassen.

Henrik Wergeland was the pioneer of modern Norwegian literature. Many succeeding writers became better known outside Norway than he did: Henrik Ibsen, Bjørnstjerne Bjørnson, Alexander Kielland, Jonas Lie, Arne Garborg, Knut Hamsun, Sigrid Undset, but of these only Ibsen can be compared to Wergeland in terms of creative power and diversity. Wergeland is to Norwegian literature what Pushkin is to the Russian, Goethe to the German, Hugo to the French, Mickiewicz to the Polish, Petőfi to the Hungarian and Byron to the English. For the writers that succeeded him, and to a great extent for the reading public, he influenced the very definition of a "Norwegian writer". Ibsen's literary and political radicalism owes much to Wergeland.

In spite of this, Wergeland has never been widely read, either then or now. His educational booklets had a large public but only *Jan van Huysum's Flower-piece* and *The English Pilot* were really appreciated by the critics. His literary work was controversial. Much of it, especially his youthful poems, which culminated in *Creation, Man and Messiah,* was considered obscure by both his contemporaries and modern readers. In many ways he has suffered the same fate as James Joyce: everyone has heard of him, but almost no one has read him.

Wergeland's grave in Vår Frelser's Gravlund lies on the top of a small rise, not far from the graves of Ibsen, Bjørnson and Munch. The best time to visit it is on a mild, light evening in May, when the scent of lilacs perfumes the air and the song of the blackbird drowns the hum of the city beyond the railings. In 1847 a monument was erected on the grave by "grateful Jews outside the borders of Norway". It is still to be seen, painted green and gold – colours decidedly more moving than beautiful – with its dedication to: "the tireless fight for human rights and the rights and freedoms of the citizen".

Acknowledgement

The translations of the following poems are based on translations by G. M. Gathorne-Hardy, Jethro Bithell and Illit Grøndahl, first published in *Henrik Wergeland. Poems*, Gyldendal Norsk Forlag, Oslo 1929:

My Little Rabbit
To a Young Poet
To a Pine-Tree
The First Butterfly
The First Time
The First Embrace
The Army of Truth
The Three
Christmas Eve
On the Sick-Bed
Follow the Call!
Second Night in the Hospital
To Spring
To my Wallflower

Het i det Stille vugang por mig
og kjærligt Vindu aabrer sig,
naar Dagene er før holdt mig bleven
før Sdræn er paa Isøen dreven.

Henr Wergeland

IVER B. NEUMANN

Wergeland in the Norwegian Political Tradition

Introduction

A traditional aspect of anniversary celebrations is to discuss whether the great men and women of the past are still of public importance today. It is a task beset with snares, particularly where authors and poets are concerned, for it is based on the idea that the broad social and political reception of the author in question takes precedence over the literary reception of his or her texts. Daniel Haakonsen, a key Wergeland scholar, was right when he argued that no particular group of people had the right to monopolise Henrik Wergeland, and that doing so would be an unworthy way to treat a poet.[2] If the poet's work is limited to that of the propagandist, he is simply not worthy to be called a poet. Furthermore, the social space in which he propagandises (if, like Wergeland, he chooses to do so), the causes for which he does so, and the language in which he does it are clearly different from those of today. The Russian formalist scholar Osip Brik, was (perhaps intentionally) wrong

---

[2] Daniel Haakonsen *Skabelsen i Henrik Wergelands diktning.* Oslo: Cappelen, 1951, p. 16.

when he remarked that if the great Russian poet Alexander Pushkin had not written *Eugene Onegin* someone else would have.

However, in spite of the snares, it is a necessary task to ask questions about an author's social importance, since there is no such thing as reading a text with no context. The author's situation, the reader's situation and the accumulation of the readings that lie between will necessarily colour any new reading. True, strong forces make for continuity. Literary genre is such a force. Furthermore, while the social sphere impinges strongly on our lives, it is not the only sphere within which we move; the physiological and psychological spheres are also central to human life, and they make for continuity between us and former generations. Social analysis must know its place, particularly where literature is concerned. Thus the more central the author has been to social and political life, the greater the snares and the more important the task. In the case of Henrik Wergeland, he is so central to Norwegian nation-building that two centuries of viewing him as a "founding father" are a daunting precedent for anyone assigned the task of assessing his importance today.

There are good reasons for Wergeland's central place in Norwegian nation-building. Under the rules of the nation-building game as they emerged in 19th-century Europe, every nation had to prove its cultural mettle. If it could not demonstrate that it had outgrown the stages of savagery and barbarism and had met what in legal parlance was referred to as the "standard of civilisation", the human collective in question was regarded as something less than a historical nation. Liberalism and Marxism alike held that only historical nations could be political nations with a right to their own state. This meant that having high culture was a necessity, which in turn, meant that nation-builders needed to be able to point to at least one great representative of all the major sciences and arts and claim him for their nation. The rules stated that a nation needed a "defining" author. In the Norwegian case, Wergeland was one of a very few candidates for the author slot, since there was little Norwegian literature to speak of before him.

But why choose Wergeland?[3] A key reason seems to be that many if not most of his contemporary colleagues had a political allegiance to a rival nation-building project, namely that of Scandinavianism. Although Wergeland was not much appreciated in the decades immediately after his death in 1845, by the 1880s he had become *the* Norwegian author. As such, he became a member of two exclusive groups. First, he stood alongside the composer Edvard Grieg and the painter I.C. Dahl as the spearheads of tradition in Norwegian culture. Second, he joined Runeberg in Finland, Petőfi in Hungary, Mickiewicz in Poland and, to mention a better-known example, Pushkin in Russia as authors who were pressed into service by nations who felt the need to present (or, in the case of Russia, strengthen) their credentials. Placing these authors in the larger social scheme of things guaranteed a focused, interested reception

---

[3] To many, it would seem a reasonable assumption that literary quality alone should be a criterion. This is definitely the case in the sense that his contemporaries would have had to recognise such quality, but later generations would not necessarily agree. For example, Wergeland's successor as key literary nation-building asset was Bjørnstierne Bjørnson, whose place in the Norwegian literary canon is already highly questionable.

of their work for as long as the nation was key to social and political life. However, such a reputation may prove to be an albatross around the neck of any great man or woman once nation-building takes on a more peripheral role in the life of a society. Trying, perhaps, to make a virtue of necessity, I will tackle the task of assessing Wergeland's contemporary importance by way of a review of how he was made a key asset by Norwegian 19th-century nation-builders.

Wergeland's Norway

In Norway, which had next to no nobility and where noble privileges were abolished in 1821, the leading stratum, which consisted of 300–400 families and which during the 19th century made up around one per cent of the population, were the etatists, known quite literally as the upper element *(embedsstanden* or *øvrigheten,* from the common Norwegian and English word 'over').[4] It was a permeable stratum, whose core consisted of 17th-century immigrant families, but which had consistently recruited bright young men from the common class *(almuen)*. Henrik Wergeland's father, Nicolai Wergeland, had arrived in typical fashion. He was of peasant stock, and had made the class journey into the upper element by dint of studying theology and being

---

4 See Iver B. Neumann 'State and Nation in the 19th Century: Recent Research on the Norwegian Case' *Scandinavian Journal of History* 2000, 25 (2): 239-260; 'This Little Piggy Stayed at Home: Why Norway is not a Member of the EU' pp. 88-129 in Lene Hansen & Ole Wæver (eds.) *European Integration and National Identity. The Challenge of the Nordic States* London: Routledge, 2002.

appointed to the state position of Lutheran pastor by the king in Copenhagen. This was one of the three normal ways of climbing the social ladder, the other two being by way of a legal education or via the officer corps. Wergeland's father's class credentials were consolidated by his marriage to a woman from one of the old families.

Nicolai Wergeland was also a writer. His book was basically a catalogue of all the dreadful things the Danes had done during Norway's four-hundred-year long history as part of the Danish composite state. It was published in 1816, and secured him a place in Norwegian history.

Norway's history as a land ruled from Copenhagen came to an abrupt end when, in 1814, Europe's great powers decided to award Norway to Sweden as compensation for Finland, which had been lost to Russia five years before. Amidst the general confusion of 1814, the upper element organised a convention which included representatives of the farmers and which succeeded in drawing up a constitution for the country. The new Swedish king, a Frenchman whose place in French politics rested on his liberal, constitutional credentials, decided to accept a watered-down version of the constitution, which meant that Norway became a state in its own right under the Swedish king.

Nicolai Wergeland's book was important because it marked a break with the upper stratum's story of what Norway was. This story, which at the time was the prevailing one, centred on the importance of the state. The general idea was that Norway, like other European states, was a project of progress. The nation was understood as the subjects of the king. The subjects fell into two major, hierarchically ordered, categories – the upper stratum and the rest. It was the upper stratum who led its charges, the people, and it did so by dint of having arrived at a higher level of civilisation in terms of refined mores and reflection. Henrik Wergeland's father diverged from this story in two important ways. First, by criticising what the Danish influence had done to Norway, he questioned whether the composite state had been a positive or even the main influence in Norwegian history. Secondly, having disposed of the state as the key civilising influence, he substituted a new historical subject for the state. This subject was the people.

Wergeland's father's move was typical of his time, and he was not alone in making it. It is, after all, a key political move away from the Enlightenment way of thinking about politics towards the Romantic way of thinking about it. It involved nothing less than a new approach to history, about who propelled history forward, and about the status and relationships of the entities of political life. Small wonder then, that for the next half-century the debate between the etatists and the Romantic Nationalists dominated Norwegian political life. The whole of Henrik Wergeland's life (1808–1845) took place within this half-century, and it was marked through and through by the political struggle between the two groups. Being his father's son, Henrik grew up with this struggle. Literary historians debate whether Wergeland can be best understood as a carryover from the Enlightenment or as a Romantic. Given that his father was a potential Norwegian Romantic and that he himself a pioneer of the Romantic literary breakthrough, the result seems moot. There is no such thing as a clean break with the past. New phenomena must grow out of something, which means that the debate about the degree to which they are new (constitute a break) or old (rooted in continuity) can never end. What may be said about Wergeland the literary figure, may also be said about Wergeland the political figure. The two ways of thinking – Enlightenment and Romanticism in literature, etatism and Romantic Nationalism in politics – exist uneasily side by side in his works.

Some key examples will suffice. Take the question of civilisation itself. To the Enlightenment, which was a French project, it was a concept in the singular. Only one civilisation existed, and different individuals and peoples took part in it in varying degrees. It went without saying that the French upper classes, and particularly the French philosophers who nurtured the concept, were to be found at the apex of civilization. To the Romantics, on the other hand, the reigning noun for the history of philosophy and social life was not civilisation but cultures, and they used it in the plural, not in the singular. Humanity was understood as existing in clusters, each cluster held together by its way of life. Each cluster had its own logic, its own recipe for the good life, its own culture. Now in Wergeland's writings we find elements of both these ways of thinking. The dominating theme is the Romantic notion that each culture follows its own logic, and Wergeland's main interest was to work for and contribute to the life of the Norwegian nation. To Wergeland, "No one may be a citizen of two states ... No one may defend two fatherlands." Furthermore, minorities should not have any exclusive collective rights, but should live their public life according to the laws and mores underwritten by the majority.[5] Against this, consider Wergeland's reasoning some months later, in the same political context, to the effect that 'civilisation' was a more enlightened ideal than the will of the people, and indeed served, and should serve, as a not-yet-realised ideal for the latter.[6] Or consider the reminiscences about his trip to France, written only three years later. Here he depicts himself as a "barbarian" visitor, who "felt a Frenchman's blood in my veins since I had set foot in that country, which I loved most after my own. *'Vive l'Armée française!'* I cry … *'Vive le drapeau tricolore!'*"[7] It is consistent with Romantic thinking that the French nation is understood as a separate entity. On the other hand, the theme of the barbarian entering the realm of France and paying allegiance to its national symbols may also be read as a carryover from the many stories told during the Enlightenment about how France held up the torch of civilisation to light the way for lesser parts of humanity. The Romantic organic understanding of the nation as a naturalised and even mystic entity sits uneasily with the Enlightenment understanding of the nation as a particular detachment of humanity gathered together in a

---

[5] The examples are from Wergeland's argumentation in favour of opening Norway's borders to Jews 1841–1842, see Odd Arvid Storsveen, *En bedre vår. Henrik Wergeland og norsk nasjonalitet* Oslo: Oslo University, 2004, on p. 695. Wergeland also had a clear assimilationist ambition, arguing, for example, that if only 'the Jew' were treated in a true Christian spirit, 'he would soon be transformed into a Christian'; *ibid.,* p. 146.

[6] *Ibid.,* p. 711. *In casu,* this was Wergeland's reaction to what he saw as the people's lack of liberal spirit; of the 43 representatives to the Storting who blocked his suggestion to lift the ban on Jews entering the country in 1842, 32 were farmers; *ibid.,* p. 710.

[7] Henrik Wergeland: *Hassel-Nødder,* pp. 241–379 in *Henrik Wergelands skrifter.* Folkeutgaven, vol. 8. Oslo: Cappelen, ([1845] 1962, p. 313.

state under the tutelage of an elite whose position is due to its high level of civilisation.

Another example of this duality is to be found in Wergeland's contributions to the key debate about who was to count as a proper Norwegian. To the etatists, anyone who was born in Norway was unquestionably a Norwegian. Beginning in the late 18th century, however, the question of who qualified as a proper Norwegian had become a major bone of contention. Wergeland was a mainstay in the growing movement which held that, in order to qualify as a Norwegian, having been born in the country was not necessarily enough. The longer your family had lived there, the better your Norwegian credentials. Wergeland employed this typically Romantic way of thinking in his political writing as well as in his frequent personal polemics with others, whom he did not hesitate to brand as foreign.[8] On the other hand, a key building block of Wergeland's politics was the idea that anyone living within a state and following its laws should be a citizen. For example, and accordingly, one of the things for which Wergeland is best remembered is his campaign against the article in the Norwegian Constitution that denied Jews and Jesuits entry to the realm. Such a playing down of what we would now call ethnicity, as well as of creed (Norway being staunchly Protestant), is a typical trait of the Enlightenment, a trait which runs directly counter to the Romantic's insistence on seeing the nation as the foundation of political life.

A third example concerns Wergeland's relationship with nature. Having grown up in the countryside, he was

---

[8] A key example being his arch-enemy Praëm; see, for example, *ibid.* p. 260.

The Meeting of the Storting, 10th February 1824. Caricature by Henrik Wergeland.

a keen observer of natural life. It would probably be an exaggeration to call him a naturalist, but he certainly shared the 18th-century penchant for studying and classifying natural phenomena. On the other hand, there is no doubt that his understanding of nature was the Romantic one of de-differentiating the divide between nature and culture in favour of an organic understanding of the human condition in general.

Norway's Wergeland

One of the very few things that has *not* been said about Henrik Wergeland is that he was a consensus-builder. He excelled in making enemies out of old friends and acquaintances, and this in a social setting where anyone who was anyone knew not only one another, but also one another's families. By the time he died of pneumonia at the age of 37, Wergeland had basically run out of people to argue with. Yet it is a highly endearing trait of his that in these quarrels, which, in typical small-town fashion, were often spawned by quibbling, there is no trace whatsoever of tactical considerations. He quarrelled with everybody – the King and the street boy, the brother-in-law and the man at the next restaurant table, the soldier on horseback leaning over him with his sabre raised, and his erstwhile most intimate collaborator. Some of these quarrels went on for decades. Wergeland lived a very public life, and most of his quarrels were public affairs. Many of them even played themselves out in the newspapers. As a result, the number of polemical texts written by Wergeland when in the throes of some strong emotion (usually anger) is so large that anyone looking for a quote will not have to look far before a fitting phrase crops up. Another result of Wergeland's quarrelsome writing career was that most people were glad to see him gone. His name was not often mentioned in the first two decades following his death.[9]

---

9 Sigurd Aa. Aarnes *"Og nevner vi Henrik Wergelands navn"* Oslo: Universitetsforlaget, 1991. What follows draws heavily on this work.

Basically, what interest there was in him at this time came from one man. He edited a collected edition of Wergeland's works in the 1850s, and penned the first biography in the 1860s. This man, Hartvig Lassen, was a typical etatist. The rather hagiographical biography focused on the parts of Wergeland's life and work that related to the Enlightenment, as this appealed most to Lassen. Wergeland's Romanticism was denied, and the parts that were undeniable were said to be due to youthful exuberance. So was Wergeland's debating style.

During the following two decades, interest in Wergeland exploded, but now the focus was on his Romantic leanings. The 1870s and the 1880s witnessed a sea-change in Norwegian society. If there is one period when the parameters of modern Norwegian politics were laid down, this was it. For example, an examination of 20th-century Norwegian ideas about war and peace will show that ideas which emerged in this period formed a bedrock for political debate to such a degree that they are easily recognisable even today, when they have become political common sense.[10] Such a colonisation of the future was made possible, among other things, by a standardisation of the stories that people told one another about the past. Historical standardisations are always the result of political and semantic struggles, where storytellers make use of disparate resources and where one story wins over others. In the case of Wergeland, as in most other cases in Norway, the etatists

---

[10] For war, see Ståle Ulriksen *Den norske forsvarstradisjonen. Militærmakt eller folkeforsvar?* Oslo: Pax, 2002; for peace, see Halvard Leira "Hele vort Folk er naturlige og fødte Fredsvenner, Norsk fredstenkning fram til 1906" *Historisk Tidskrift* 2004 83 (2): 153–180.

lost the argument. The following quote from Wergeland's biographer Lassen expresses the gist of the matter:

Politically, of course he [Wergeland] expected everything from the people; but he did not expect it from a murky 'people's instinct' (as Mr B. Bjørnson [Wergeland's self-proclaimed poet successor] calls it), but from a people raised and educated for self government; and this is something very different from this people's ignorance, which is now the subject of so much pontification about town.[11]

It was at this historical juncture that Wergeland was installed as national poet.[12] The fact that the 1870s and 1880s were such important years in Norwegian nation-building is not only due to urbanisation and the making of a working class, but also with the arrival in political life of a radical populist position which potentially had broad support and which therefore had to be accommodated in one way or another. Up to this point, the etatists had ruled the roost in Norwegian political life. The Romantic Nationalists who had made up the idealistic opposition had, as we have seen, come from the same elite of civil service families as the etatists, and they had at least to some degree shared the etatist notion that it was the historical mission of the civil service stratum to educate and civilise the people. To the Romantic Nationalists, the people were an object of fascination, something to be

---

[11] Quoted in Aarnes, p. 83.

[12] *Ibid*. Storsveen 2004, p. 660, rightly points out that Wergeland's attempt to forge a specifically Norwegian national literature actually failed, and that it was only realised decades later.

studied and intermittently adored, but also something which had little agency, and which should definitely not be left to make its own, unguided decisions. Wergeland's view that 'civilisation' was a more enlightened ideal than the will of the people betrayed not only his Enlightenment outlook, it was also connected with a socially based tension within the Romantic Nationalist position itself. It is indicative of the social level on which Wergeland carried out his nation-building that what he became justly remembered for was his work in the realm of national symbols and ritual, namely the celebration of 17 May as the national day. This is supposed to be the day on which the Constitution was adopted in 1814, but the constitutional draft which was drawn up on that date was never implemented. This underlines how it was the symbolic, and not the practical, level of national life that turned out to be Wergeland's home ground. Given that Wergeland was a poet, this should not be surprising; nonetheless, it was not to become a key insight about Wergeland until his reception took a political turn one hundred years later, at the end of the 20th century.

The new populist position that came into its own in the 1870s and 1880s wanted to do away with the tutelage of the civil servants. Where the Wergelands and the other civil service Romantic Nationalists had seen the Danish cultural influences that hampered Norwegian nation-building as a set of cultural practices that could and should be shorn away, the populists tended to hold that it was the civil servant class *as such* which prevented the Norwegian people from coming into its own. There were certain problems with this position. Moral considerations aside, it was not practicable to expel families who had lived in Norway for two hundred years and more, particularly as they possessed an abundance of social and cultural skills that were needed to run the country and as the populists had no way of replacing them, at least in the short term. However, in political terms, the populists could speak on behalf of the people with a lot more weight than the Romantic Nationalists could. They were 'of the people' themselves and their knowledge of the people came from personal experience. But political life was still in the hands of the civil servants. The situation called for accommodation and compromise. In particular, it was important to tell stories about Norway which gave it a continuous history and which made it seem that nation-building was a "natural" process whereby ever new groups could join what was presented as being basically one continuous process.

Wergeland was eminently fitted for this social and political situation. Like his father, he had been a vocal opponent of Danish cultural influence. That he also saw Danish influence as a civilising contribution to Norwegian history was ignored. His key political project had been to exhort new groups – basically farmers, but also workers – to acquire the assets necessary to participate in political life and to qualify as voters. He had also spent a lot of energy on opening the country to a new group of another kind, namely the Jews. That he was also a vocal opponent of women's participation in social and political life was likewise ignored.[13]

The upshot was that Wergeland was cast as a forerunner of the coalition of Romantic Nationalists and populists who took over Norwegian political life during the

---

[13] See Storsveen 2004, pp. 627 and 665–666.

1880s. In the early decades of the 20th century this coalition was also the hothouse of ideas for much of the Norwegian workers' movement. The historian and sometime foreign minister Halvdan Koht, a mainstay of Norwegian political and cultural life from the end of the 19th century and into the 1950s, was one of those who found their way from this coalition to the working class movement without changing his social and political ideas in any basic way. Once the revolutionary wing of the workers' movement had been marginalised within the Labour Party from the early 1930s onwards, it was the ideas from the 1880s and 1890s on which the party based its platform. Thus Wergeland's role as the predecessor of the Romantic and populist nationalist coalition, which became dominant in Norwegian political life 50 years after the 1880s, could continue unchanged, but he had now become the predecessor's predecessor.

The nature of Wergeland's popularity underwent certain changes over the years. When his reputation as a national figure was at its height, the flame was kept alight by a core of historians and literary historians, and his texts were broadly used in school curricula as well as in speeches and celebratory poems recited at public gatherings, particularly on 17 May. However, from the early decades of the 20th century, appreciation of Wergeland took an aesthetic, scholarly turn, which by mid-century had superseded the nation-building one. The school curriculum was the next to go. Whereas in my father's (b. 1914) school days Wergeland was such a household name that parodying his style was a popular pastime ('Oh! You little piece of rope in my trouser pocket!'), my own experience (b. 1959) was that Wergeland was taught en passant, his poems only appealing to those of

us who already had literary leanings. Part of this was due to the way in which the Labour Party was making upper secondary education available to the mass of the people, divesting the curriculum of most of its historical features in the process, but it was also due to a deliberate playing down of Wergeland's importance.[14] A concurrent, and probably consequential, drop in the use of Wergeland in connection with 17th May followed, although his name is still regularly invoked in the many speeches that are delivered throughout the country on this day.

Wergeland Today

It is not what Henrik Wergeland said, but how he said it, that earned him his central place in the history of Norwegian nation-building. Since he was a writer, our appreciation of him must in the final instance be based on his texts. However, his colossal production, even the belletrist part, is highly uneven, and much of it is falling into oblivion. No matter. His place in Norwegian literary history is secured by poems about aspects of the human condition which may have different manifestations, but whose base is physiological; they will definitely not disappear within the foreseeable future (birth, copulation and death, as T.S. Eliot would have put it).

Wergeland's place in Norwegian political history is equally secure, and is currently the object of a new wave of research, some of which I have drawn on when writing this article. Wergeland was for many years held up to school pupils as a great Norwegian and an exemplary human being, but if appreciation of his person and his work is to

---

[14] Cf. Aarnes 1991, p. 136.

continue, this version will have to be somewhat revised. His incendiary views and stubborn and quarrelsome character were given free reign for all to see. He probably never slept with a woman from his own social stratum. When he died, the only person whose friendship he had been able to keep over time was his own father's.[15] In short, he seems to have been deficient in quite ordinary human skills. All this notwithstanding, I think there are two axes along which Wergeland will still be remembered in the years to come.

The first of these is his political campaign in favour of opening Norway to Jews. Of course, Wergeland's arguments cannot be transposed to present-day conditions. It was a key point for him that the Jews did not have their own state, and he insisted that they and other self-conscious minorities were not entitled to special treatment. He had assimilationist leanings. It would be thoroughly ahistorical to enlist him as a supporter of one or the other side in debates on Palestinian rights, immigration or present-day Norwegian legislation. Part of the reason why Wergeland's role in the admission of Jews to Norway is still justly celebrated is of course related to his willingness to ask whether there are voices that are not being heard in the social and political debate, and whether there are groups that are not even in a position to have a voice. Regardless of his own patchy application of this idea, this is where Wergeland's characteristic mix of Enlightened and Romantic energies still speaks to us. Like Immanuel Kant, a philosopher who wrote at the same historical juncture but whose works he does not seem to have been conversant with, he held it to be a duty for each

---

[15] Compare Storsveen 2004, p. 543.

and every one of us to open our doors to strangers in need. And with reference to another philosopher, Wergeland fits Richard Rorty's recipe for how writers can play a key political role by evoking the reader's sympathy with new groups of people simply by driving home these people's humanity. In Wergeland's writings, humanity emerges as a political project, but one that has to take a back seat to other, more specific political projects. I would argue that our efforts to grapple with this dilemma also lie at the heart of present-day political life, this time as a global challenge.

The second axis along which Wergeland remains politically relevant is as a type of presence in the political debate. Wergeland never ran for political office. He did make the occasional suggestion for a legislative amendment, but this was definitely a side issue for him. He generally left it to others to work out the practical details. Wergeland's chosen role was that of the critic, the man who rushed in where angels feared to tread in order to speak (or perhaps one should say "blurt out") truth to power. These truths were definitely his own, and were not necessarily shared by anyone else, and they were often uttered at considerable social and political risk to himself. Wergeland was a great exponent of fearless speech. He belongs to the tradition of those whom the Greeks called *parrhesiastes,* people who make it their business to speak truth to power regardless of the danger they may run in doing so. There is also a parrhesiast quality to the way in which Wergeland disregarded not only the consequences, but also the ornamental and ritual parts of public performance. Many parrhesiasts made it a point to shock their audiences. Intentionally or not, Wergeland's attacks on social and political life usually had the same effect.

The *parrhesiastes* were the predecessors of the modern critical intellectuals.[16] I have already emphasised that Wergeland has been placed in a whole plethora of traditions, and that he does not fit completely into any of them. I should therefore point out that there are also problems with seeing Wergeland as a parrhesiast. He was, after all, a man who lived on the King's shilling in his final years. But then again, any social classification breaks down if it is scrutinised carefully enough. The Wergeland of tradition is a bowdlerised version, a clean-shaven and nationalistically right-thinking figure. The time has come to take the opposite tack and draw attention to his wild side, which, there is ample proof, was a very important, if not the predominant, part of the man.

---

[16] See Foucault, Michel (2001) (ed. Joseph Pearson) *Fearless Speech*, New York, NY: Semiotext(e).

METTE LENDING

My Wergeland

Translated from the Norwegian by Anna Paterson

In 1819, the eleven-year-old Henrik Wergeland left home – the parsonage in Eidsvoll – and moved to Christiania,[17] where he was to be a pupil at the city's ancient cathedral school (katedralskole). He passed his school-leaving examinations in 1825, enrolled at Norway's first university – the Royal Fredrik University (Kongelige Fredriks Universitet), founded in 1811 – and went on to graduate in theology.

In Wergeland's day, the cathedral school occasionally served as the gathering place for the Norwegian national assembly, the Storting. After the Storting had taken over the building for good in 1823, the school changed its address several times before finally settling, in 1902, in the building on Ullevålsveien which houses it today. In that same year, women pupils were admitted for the first time. Over a century later, the composition of the student body proves that other social and cultural barriers have now been breached. In Wergeland's time, the school was the preserve of sons of professional men, but nowadays it attracts pupils with varying ethnic and religious backgrounds, and from every social class.

---

[17] The capital city, later renamed Oslo.

118

Why are ambitious young people from every corner of Oslo applying to Wergeland's old school by preference? How do the pupils of today relate to one of their greatest predecessors and his lasting fame?

Here, three young women speak of how the presence of Henrik Wergeland is still felt in Oslo Katedralskole – or "Katta", as it is commonly known – and how much the ideals he fought for all his life, especially in his writing, still matter today.

Abida Rasheed (17) is about to begin her last year at the school. She says:

"Not many people from my lower secondary school applied to Katta. But I had heard so many positive things about the school before I started there. Somehow, everyone is aware that the pupils are really smart and committed – people who know what they want and are determined to reach whatever goals they've set themselves. I knew too that Katta was a well-run school with good teachers and proper discipline. Of course, I also knew that, over the years, quite a few famous people had studied here – not just Henrik Wergeland, but also other people who were important in Norway's history. I guess you might say this school is a prestigious place.

"I was just a little girl when I heard about Wergeland, probably in connection with celebrating 17th May[18] and the children's parade. Later on, in secondary school, I got to know more about Wergeland as a *person* and realised what a wide range of causes he was engaged in. He was

---

[18] Norway's National Day – cf. Footnote 20.

fired up by so many different issues! We had this really keen Norwegian teacher who taught us a lot about Wergeland – not just the poet, but also the man and the citizen. And, no question about it, an enthusiastic teacher makes almost all the difference... Since then I've come across Wergeland in biographies, but never studied his work in depth. All the same, I feel he's somehow familiar. It's so easy to become charmed by him – and fall a little in love with him as a person, if you see what I mean.

"We, the Katta pupils, have a tradition of laying a wreath

on his grave on 17th May. The cemetary of Vår Frelsers Gravlund is of course right across the street from the school and we often go there in connection with the teaching as well. As far as I can remember Wergeland didn't get very good marks in maths or science, but he was good at Greek, Latin, history and geography. I actually read somewhere that he was very close to his teachers in these subjects.

"*The* quality I associate with Henrik Wergeland is political engagement. He was so involved in the new union between Norway and Sweden and the relationship between the two countries. Maybe it wasn't so strange, given that his father was one of the "Men of Eidsvoll"[19]. After all, because his father was the pastor there, Wergeland grew up in Eidsvoll, for a while anyway. I see him as a man totally devoted to social progress. You can see it in his poetry too, because it's often full of references to politics. Wergeland was ahead of his time in many ways and much of what he wrote must have seemed very provocative to his contemporaries – just look at his love poems, which are so frank and direct.

"Otherwise, well, he had studied theology – I suppose he was preoccupied with religion in general. As far as I can remember, he had controversial views about Christianity too. He returns to the relationships between the different religions in many of his works. It seems he thought that, basically, most religions are quite alike. Didn't he suggest that, when everything was said and done, we have one God in common? Anyway, I think that's what he writes in *Creation, Man and Messiah,* like when he says there is one

---

[19] Eidsvoll was the site of an early medieval regional ting (assembly). The Men of Eidsvoll drafted the first Norwegian Constitution, signed on 17th May, 1814.

spirit, or soul – a world-soul – that is present everywhere. To Wergeland, this soul was identical to God. Though naturally he was very aware at the same time that there are huge distinctions to be made between faiths. Still, I'm sure that Wergeland cared a great deal for all kinds of different people. It follows that he saw how important it is to be tolerant.

"If Wergeland had lived today, he would surely have been involved in the question of Norway's relationship with the European Union. Of course it's impossible to be certain, one way or the other, but I believe he might've been against Norwegian membership – he was always very keen on maintaining Norway's independence and its status as a full partner in the union. But his engagement would hardly have been limited to Norwegian concerns. He really cared about other countries and other population groups. For one thing, I'm positive he would have followed in detail what has been happening in the Middle East. Generally speaking, he always backed the weak in the community, wanting to help the small, oppressed people. That's why I feel sure that he would've been all for supporting the fight against poverty and the efforts to get the relationship between North and South right. He would've fought for a fairer distribution of global resources. Just to pick one organisation, his goals were very like Amnesty's: justice, equality and universal human rights – at least, these are the values I connect with him.

"It's hard to think of anyone alive today who is like Wergeland. The only one who comes to mind is a former prime minister, Kjell Magne Bondevik. What I mean is that both men have that special intensity, they are both very engaged in promoting social justice and supporting the weak in society and things like that. And Bondevik, like Wergeland, studied theology. He was probably a calmer kind of person, though. Bondevik uses other ways of working than Wergeland, of course – but their social engagement seems just as strong.

"Wergeland went a little wild sometimes. He had such energy. It must have been great to be around him, but maybe a bit exhausting now and then? He was such a strong character. One of these people who never give in – the kind of person who always stands up for what he believes in and never betrays his ideals. But he was also a romantic, a dreamer, someone who was dreaming about what was unattainable and longing for what he could not have. He was a poet in love with nature and could make anything come alive: trees, flowers, springtime, the sky ... Wergeland had so many sides to his personality – he cared very deeply about so many areas of life – and it's surely exactly this quality which makes reading his work today so satisfying.

"It's really hard to imagine that someone as alive and vigorous as Wergeland would ever have become old and conservative. He was who he was, impulsive and unpredictable. He never allowed himself to be cowed by anyone or anything. To me, he was like a Jack-in-the-box – someone who pops out suddenly and surprises you, before disappearing again to think and write about new causes to fight for.

"I think Wergeland would have enjoyed being at Katta now. At least he would've found it varied and open to new ideas and welcoming all kinds of people. Besides, in his day, it was a boys-only school – and Wergeland was rather fond of women, wasn't he? If I were to wish for something to celebrate Wergeland's bicentenary, it would be that there was more time to study him at school, as a writer and poet, and as a person too. Then Norwegian pupils today would become as familiar with Henrik Wergeland as they are, for instance, with Henrik Ibsen."

Catharina Broch (18) has just completed her work for *examen artium*.[20] She says:

"I was the only one from my lower secondary school who went on to Katta – in my year, anyway. I applied to go there because it is a good school with excellent teachers. Besides, I definitely wanted to have a chance to meet people from everywhere in town and avoid being stuck in a setting where everyone was alike.

"During Norwegian lessons, the teachers often made a point of mentioning that Henrik Wergeland had been at our school. I had heard quite a few stories about him and many of them were about the mischief he got up to. Once, one of the teachers let us see some of his old reports, the subject marks as well. As far as I can remember, the marks weren't that good. But maybe it was because Henrik had lived on his own in digs since he was thirteen? I think he stayed with an uncle during the two first years at Katta, but that the uncle was so strict Henrik couldn't put up with living there for very long.

"My father has been interested in Wergeland for ages and quotes him now and then. He has told me a great deal about Wergeland's life and work, and has taken me to see many of the places in Oslo that have a connection to his life – Grotten, for instance, and Damstredet and the stable

---

[20] Final school-leaving examinations.

for his horse Vesle-Brunen.[21] It's fair to say that I've grown up with Wergeland. We've also visited Eidsvoll quite a few times on 17 May. That's the place where the family lived after Nikolai Wergeland, the father, had become the local pastor. As it happens, my great-great-great-grandfather was a Man of Eidsvoll in 1814, just like Henrik's father.

---

[21] Damstredet is a street where Wergeland lived. Grotten is the house which Wergeland let build near the Royal Palace in 1841, and which he was forced to sell shortly before his death in 1845. Today it serves as an honorary residence – currently inhabited by Norwegian composer Arne Nordheim.

"I suppose my mother, who's Polish, isn't such a great fan of Wergeland, not like my father. But she too agrees that there are few people of his stature in the history of the world and that we have every reason to feel proud of him. He was a poet of genius and at the same time a good man, who fought with passion on behalf of the weak in society.

"It was probably Dad who suggested that I should study Henrik Wergeland for my special subject essay. Anyway, I decided to examine Wergeland's views on the arts – his ideas about the role of the poet and of art in general – and to focus on how well he lived up to his own ideals. I knew from the start that his dominant approach to life was that of a Romantic. He thought of the artist as a seer, a visionary, who could perceive and communicate eternal truths. The artist had a duty to make this a better world.

"When I worked on the background to my special subject, I started from three poems: "To a Young Poet", "Follow the Call!" and *Jan van Huysum's Flower-piece* and read some of the biographies as well, which was quite good fun – he did such a lot of exceptional things. And my conclusion was rather unsurprising: he really was "the lightning herald-hurled",[22] just he felt the artist should. It's a fact that many of the ideas that he felt particularly strongly about have gained acceptance after his time.

"Studying Wergeland seriously almost makes one fall a little in love with him. He threw himself into so many causes, selflessly and without personal motives, and he stood up for people in need – he was a true idealist. Another

---

[22] From "To a Young Poet": the poet is spoken of as a seer and poetry as the flash of lightning that lights up the sky ahead of the thunder: "et foranskudt lyn".

thing about him was his incredible learning. His style demands a lot from the reader, what with all the metaphors he used and all the references to works of art and people we don't know much about nowadays. It seems that his contemporaries too regarded him as a little inaccessible, but in the main that was probably because Wergeland was so far ahead of his time and in favour of ideas that were unfamiliar to most people. But he was also an outstanding popular educator and very good at getting his message across.

"It's true that Wergeland was regarded as quite a trying character: he held strong opinions about so many things. I've read somewhere that, when he was talking, it was often in a monologue rather than a dialogue. And being confrontational didn't worry him at all. Didn't he who write something like "Pain makes the heart grow stronger / battle hardens the arm / in a storm the voice is louder".[23] I assume he meant that struggling against resistance can make you stronger. He had many obstacles to overcome himself, both in his love life and in his attempts to find permanent work – but, as a rule, it seems that he was able to see something positive in everything, even his problems.

"If he had been alive today, he would've been fighting for all sorts of things – not just on behalf of people, but of animals too. That's what I think, anyway. He was very concerned about all living things and his poetry is characterised by metaphors drawn from nature. It's easy to imagine him engaged in animal protection issues, from keeping pets

---

[23] "Hjertet styrkes ved at lide,/ Armens Muskler ved at stride,/ Stemmen heves i en Blest".

and animal experimentation to chicken farming and the use of fur in the fashion industry.

"Anyway, I also think he would have worked to further democracy and human rights, at both national and international level. Even though Wergeland cared so much about conditions in Norway, he was concerned about what happened outside the borders of this country as well. In the first verse of his poem "The Spokesman for the Common People of Norway" (Den norske almuestalsmann) he writes: "The hottest flame in the Norseman's soul/ burns with hatred of tyrants, large and small"[24] – and that was surely as typical of him as of anyone. He was so concerned about the weak and oppressed. For instance, I know he wrote about freedom for the Poles. He wouldn't have approved of the gap between the West and the deprived parts of the world, that's for sure. He would've fought for social justice and I think that he would have been in favour of the United Nations and supranational decision-making. Amnesty's work would have appealed to him too.

"Wergeland wasn't exactly a conventional Christian. He had studied theology, but some of his views were controversial. It seems he was given a poor mark in his final exam because he argued against some of the central tenets of the teaching. The result was in any case – presumably also because of the conflicts, the kind of unfortunate things that happened – that he was never appointed to a benefice.

"Honestly, I think that Wergeland chose to study theology because of the Christian teaching that people are

---

[24] "Den heteste flamme i nordmannens indre / er hat mot tyranner, de store og mindre".

128

spiritual beings – this fitted in with his personal experience of life. Of course, his father was a clergyman too. Wergeland believed that existence and, especially, love – physical love as well – was a spiritual state. But he didn't always approve of those who acted as spokesmen for Christianity, whether they were employed by the Church or the university. Or, at least in his hard-hitting poem "The Army of Truth", he insists that these institutions – the "Temple" and the "Pillar" – are full of prejudice. In the prose Afterword to the poem "Follow the Call!" he writes about a young woman who is moved by the fate of the Jews, for instance their being forbidden from entering Norway: "[...] Once, by the heart of such a woman, He will find rest who 'shall come after' and with whom all ages will be united, like rivers merging on their way towards the sea." Here, Wergeland seems to have had a vision of the second coming of the Messiah. And there's another poem, "The Three", where Wergeland presents the Muslim, Jewish and Christian faiths as three expressions of the same God. And that isn't exactly ortho-dox Christianity, is it? The way I see it, Wergeland thought that love is what matters most in all these religions – love of humanity and all of creation."

Helene Pintzka Mendelsohn (26) has just completed her medical training and passed her examen artium in 1999. She says:

"Katta is known as the kind of school which is aware that everyone is not the same. It reaches out and offers something to everyone – and that's true when it comes to socialising as well. It's easy to find one's own niche. Besides, the school is known for its good teachers. The broad recruit-

ment base means that it's easy to find someone who shares your interests. For instance, lots of people make friends within the framework of the school theatre. I came straight from a lower secondary school that I was quite fed up with and felt badly in need of a change. For me it was really great to be in a school like Katta, which is so many-faceted and rich in resources.

"On grand occasions, the headmaster likes to refer to some of the many famous people have been pupils at Katta over the years. As for Henrik Wergeland, he's special because he is buried in Vår Frelsers Gravlund, just across the road from the school. During Norwegian periods our teacher often led the way down into cemetery and showed us the orderly rows of Norwegian writers: "Now then, here is Bjørnson, here is Ibsen – and over here is Wergeland."

"As for me, I've actually got a special relationship with Vår Frelsers Gravlund, because my family has always visited Wergeland's grave on 17th May. There's a speech given by someone representing the Organisation of Jewish Youth and then people can step forward to place their own wreaths on the grave. We have many photos of these marks of respect at home. It's usually the same members of the society – the Mosaic Religious Community – who turn up, which makes it fun and interesting to go through the pictures, because they show people you've seen there since childhood, year after year. I think it's a fine, meaningful way to begin the day, before wandering off to mingle with the crowds. Some years ago, after I had left Katta and started studying, I made the speech at this event on 17th May. The following year, my brother spoke. You might say that I've known Henrik Wergeland all my life.

"When I was little, I didn't know very much about his poetry of course. But both my parents have worked in the theatre, so I learnt lots about literature and drama at my mother's knee. My mother has taught Norwegian as well – actually, she taught at Katta – and, come to think of it, she surely read Wergeland's poems for children aloud to us children.

"All of us in the Jewish community are naturally grateful for Wergeland's great contribution to the removal of Article 2 of the Constitution, which said that Jews were not permitted to live in Norway. But he fought for many other

131

causes too. Perhaps that's why everyone finds an *individual* path leading to Wergeland – it's like, he's got something that matters to everyone.

"The thing is, Wergeland was such an *actively* caring person. He wasn't one of those who stay on the sidelines, watching injustice being done. On the contrary, he stood up for others, to a degree you rarely see nowadays. When he felt passionately about something, he fought for it, always so exceptionally eager and enthusiastic – and that was true of his poetry too. Even if things looked hopeless at times, he believed in the capacity of art to influence people.

"If Wergeland had been alive now, I'm sure he would have carried on using art to promote causes that were close to his heart. It's obviously hard to say exactly what he would've fought for. But if one's allowed to speculate…? Well, he was a romantic soul and truly fascinated by all the beautiful nature that surrounded him. In the poem "Myself", he writes among other things: "I, a man who needs but a glimpse of the sun to burst out laughing, filled with inexplicable joy …". So, doesn't it seem likely that nature would still matter to him – maybe also environmental and climate-related issues?

"But Wergeland would of course never be concerned about just one thing…! He was a champion of truth, freedom and justice – and fought against prejudice, lies and superstition. In the collection of poems called *The Jew,* he writes for instance: "Storming the ramparts of darkness is hard/ superstition rests securely on strong pillars." He wanted to make the whole world into a better place for everyone and joined battle to promote rights for the weak and poor in society.

"It is a fact that I cannot think of anyone in Norway today who can compare with Wergeland. What I mean is: of course politicians care about issues, but in a way ... that's their job. And again, there are many others who are ready to do frontline duty, but even so, Wergeland is unique. His intensity and drive showed in so many contexts and he made his mark in a wide range of different areas. It's his sheer diversity of purpose that's rare nowadays, when most people stay within their narrow specialties.

"Besides, he really did make some causes his own. He was impulsive and paid no attention to the conventional way of going about business. Take his action about Article 2, for instance: he just marched along to the Storting and delivered his documents. "Here you are! I want something done about this – now!" Then there was the way he used his art to influence people. Writing poetry was an important means for him to influence the positions taken up by decision-makers and by society at large. You can see this for example in his work to further the cause of the Jews in Norway.

"Norwegian society has changed a lot since the beginning of the 19th century, not least because it has become a more multi-cultural nation. And, of course, the more social groups, the more new problems, which Wergeland would've felt strongly about today. You still hear all the time about people who have negative experiences, but, despite that, I'd like to think that generally speaking we're now more tolerant towards people who are different. When you hear the stories from the time when the first coloured people arrived in Norway, it's easy to take on board that much has changed for the better! Though it must be said, my husband, who wears the *kippah*,[25] and I have had a few nasty

---

[25] Jewish round skullcap.

remarks come our way. Sure, society isn't ideal nowadays either. Still, most of the time what happens is that people come up to him and say things like: "Oh, you're wearing the *kippah* – that's so good! You don't see it often in Norway!"

"In my view, tolerance is closely linked to knowledge. Perhaps it would be a good idea to invest more in education, to give everyone a chance to learn more about people different from themselves. It's a fact that most of us exist in rather homogenous surroundings. We discussed it at medical school and one of my fellow students suggested, among other things, that we should be taught comparative religion as part of the medical curriculum. After all, as doctors we'll come across many patients with very different backgrounds. And to study this would surely be a project in the spirit of Wergeland? He was so deeply involved in work to enlighten people.

"Henrik Wergeland's enthusiasm and energy must have meant that he came across as a very intense personality. Being rather rebellious, even wilful, seems to have been part of his character – at least, I think it's hard to imagine him as old and set in his ways. But then, he died as quite a young man. On the other hand, thirty-seven isn't *that* young. There are many who stop getting involved in causes by the time they're twenty-five! And in his day, adult life started so much earlier. It's only nowadays that thirty-seven-year-olds regard themselves as young …"

VIGDIS YSTAD

Wergeland and Religious Tolerance
Translated from the Norwegian by Alison Arderne Philip

Wergeland had a deeply religious nature, as anyone with any knowledge of his poetry can testify. But they could also testify that his views were never dogmatic; he never claimed to put forward eternal truths concerning God. In his work he returns again and again to the mystery of the nature of God, which he felt that every sensitive and thinking person must explore.

   Wergeland's own examination of this question was based on his consciousness of a creative power that manifested itself in every living thing. He perceived every plant and creature, from the smallest to the greatest, as a sign of God's existence. This is vividly expressed in his poem "The Leaves of the Oak", written in 1840:

> In faith, believe that every hair
> Upon your head is reckoned,
> That e'en the leaf upon the tree
> Was wrought by the same hand,
> ...
> Look closely, you will see
> The great things in the small.
> The feeble stalk of grass the wing
> On which God's thoughts soar heavenwards,

...
The mown grass has sung its song;
The lichen's green-grey skin –
God's was the hand that patterned it,
Its loveliness did carve.

And in the powerful canto in "Let there be Light!", also written in 1840:

As the streams asunder part,
So there flows through every soul
A single light divine.

But who, or what, is this one divine creator? This is the subject of the major, all-encompassing work of Wergeland's youth, his dramatic poem *Creation, Man and Messiah*. It was written in 1829-30, while he was studying theology at Det kongelige Fredriks Universitet [now the University of Oslo]. Had the poem been written in one of the world languages, it would today be regarded as one of the most important works in western literature. The first part, entitled "Creation", is a forceful presentation of Wergeland's cosmogony, in which he gives an account of the creation and growth of life on our planet, which he depicts as a mere speck in an infinite universe, and maintains that behind all this there is a divine Creator. From the formless, steaming chaos of the earth arise two heavenly spirits, Ohebiel and Phun-Abiriel. The first is filled with unconditional love, the second is torn by doubt. Wergeland explains these names: Ohebiel means "loving angel" and Phun-Abiriel "the strong, brooding angel". The two spirits discuss the nature of God, a discussion that covers the relationship between God and matter, God and spirits, God and phenomena such as life and death. The dialogue is carried forward by Ohebiel's replies to the repeated questions of Phun-Abiriel, the doubter, who opens the discussion.

> What, lives this mud? I see it breathes.
> Is God then in this lump? Shall it be worshipped?
> Behold the swollen belly of the world! By what begot?

Phun-Abiriel is unable to believe in what he cannot see or explain rationally, and his lack of certainty about the goodness of an all-powerful God is eating him away. "The worm of doubt perpetual consumes me ... I am a thought in the pain of the soul of God ... Behold, Ohebiel / the mystery, gaping like a wound". But Ohebiel answers:

> Believe the world the temple is of God: this earth
> A new-raised pillar, eternity's great gate,
> Immortality's a morning-coloured dome,
> Each spirit a paean of praise that rolls
> down the pathway of eternity
> ...
> Let it suffice that all around is good.

It is a matter of interpretation whether Ohebiel has really succeeded in removing Phun-Abiriel's doubts. But the rest of the poem can be read as an unbroken demonstration of

God's infinite goodness and creative power; a stream of life wells up from the newly created earth. Wergeland also describes life in all its forms as thoughts in God's world poem, as when he introduces the figure of the Messiah, who says:

God's words are spirits: flowers that bloom from dust.
God's thoughts are worlds.
As a spirit in the meanest speck of dust, the word
Sleeps hidden in the thought.

The Messiah of the poem is not the same as the biblical Jesus; he is the highest of the spirits, and has previously lived elsewhere in the universe, on a different planet. In his revision of the poem in 1845, to which he gave the title *Man*, Wergeland called this figure Akadiel, probably to avoid misunderstanding.

But inherent in the Creation is the possibility of evil and meaninglessness, which is signified at an early stage by the brooding figure of Phun-Abiriel and becomes increasingly evident as mankind and the rest of the earth develop. I shall not explore this theme in any detail here, but will concentrate on the aspects that in a general way reflect Christian Neoplatonism and the philosophy of *Logos*.

The spirit of God is present in all things, whether great or small. Wergeland describes the evolution of life on our planet in terms of a continuous process of creation powered by divine freedom and love. Life comes into being from the unceasing stream of creative force flowing from God. It evolves in the form of a chain, which begins with the least and smallest of creatures, like the lowly earthworm, and rises higher and higher, to culminate in Man's liberating awareness. Wergeland calls this creative force "God's eternal light, which grows from an insect-gleam to a sun". But it is only man who reaches, and is granted, awareness. Because God has also given man the capacity for love and freedom, man is able with the aid of his awareness to realise the thousand-year Millennium on earth. But man constantly shows that he is unworthy of such a gift; indeed over the course of history men's memory of their spiritual origins has become fainter and fainter. This allows worldly and religious tyrants to exploit their power to deceive and oppress individuals; the clergy distort the true religion and lead men astray by preaching a religious mysticism and religious myths about nature.

During this process Jesus appears, not as God, but as the most perfect of beings. He preaches a very different message from that of the priests:

Awake, spirit, slumbering in these hearts!
See, spirit, from Heav'n your gloriousness
I bring again to dust!

Before the Earth came into being: in the beginning
You were with God, knowing the truth,
And your own nature, clear and sure
As if you were God's word that spoken, said:
You are!
And all Heav'n answered: Yes! You are!
And you delighted in the company
Of Heaven's spirits,
In truth, in love, in liberty!

Here it is the Word, knowledge in the sense of awareness, that creates. What Jesus, and the poem in general, preaches is similar to the idea that *logos,* the word, is at one and the same time divine reason and a never-ending creative power that realises itself in the cosmos and gives it order and meaning. This view is also to be found in early Greek philosophy and as such it predates Christianity.

Creation, Man and Messiah was published in 1830, the year of the July Revolution in France, and the religious ideas propounded by the young student of theology were certainly not those of orthodox Lutheranism. The concept of God set out in the poem is open and all-encompassing. The ideas and images reflect those of Platonism, Neoplatonism and Christianity. And its religious centre is the concept of a cosmic freedom and love.

After the publication of *Creation, Man and Messiah* Wergeland continued to express views on the concept of God that diverged considerably from those of the orthodox Lutheran Church of Norway. In a treatise entitled "Why does humanity progress so slowly?", published in 1831, the year after the July Revolution, Wergeland writes about the lack of consistency between the advance of political ideas and the progression of religious doctrines, an inconsistency he describes as a "fundamental evil" in men's lives. While the revolution is progressing towards political freedom, writes Wergeland, religion is moving in the opposite direction.

Wergeland maintained that human civilisation stagnates if it is governed by a dogmatic religious doctrine. The opposite situation, a total absence of religion, is equally undesirable, but European religious doctrines need to be revised.

Religion must make room for human reason. It is important to note that Wergeland is using "reason" in the Romantic sense: by virtue of their reason, human beings are God's representatives on earth; this is particularly manifested in great souls such as Socrates, Plato, Mohammed and especially Christ. Thus reason is not merely the quality shown by Phun-Abiriel, i.e. the ability to draw conclusions from the world of experience, it is also the quality of being able to come into direct contact with the spiritual world and with God. As Ågot Benterud (undated) wrote in *Henrik Wergeland's Religious Development*, "It was the same concept of reason that Rousseau used when, in *The Creed of a Priest of Savoy,* the priest says he will consult his 'inner light', meaning his own reason."

Wergeland is employing this meaning in "Why does humanity progress so slowly?", where he says that "the moral nature and educational value of a religion, what can be deduced from objective human reason, must necessarily be emphasised in a consistent system as a religion for everyone". Thus it is not primarily the priests who should mediate between earth and heaven; this can be done by the divine reason that is to be found in every individual. The priest must resume his task of educating the people.

In this article Wergeland also writes that God built Christianity out of fragments from earlier religious systems, uniting them all in perfect harmony in a pantheon "under whose dome he placed the knowledge of God and immortality taught by the wholesome dogma that is necessary for all people". But Christians have become divided and blood has flowed as much as ink between the conflicting sides. If thought and belief are liberated, men will again be aware that all religions are one: "Then we would see all enlightened Mahommedans [sic], Chinese, Hindus and Jews converted, and bring European civilisation down to their people ... then we would witness the fulfilment of Christ's prophecy that there shall be one flock with one shepherd, which is to say that all people will live like brothers; a vision of man, as he in his moral perfection manifested himself in Christ, shall rule as a living, life-giving presence in every man ... Then the improvement of political constitutions could advance without coming into conflict with religious doctrine". There would again be "one flock with one shepherd, a humanity that would strive, one for all and all for one, to achieve the vision of a perfect human being, who would ... live in all and rule all". According to Wergeland this could be achieved by reforming "enshackled religious doctrines".

In his revised version, *Man*, Wergeland introduced a new section entitled "The Spiritual Resurrection of Jesus". Here Akadiel allows the poet a glimpse of the future, in which the latter sees an earthly millennium, where church and state have separated, despots and dictators have disappeared, Christianity is no longer split into different branches, and the Greek Orthodox, Roman Catholic and Protestant churches form a new unity, free from the old dogmas:

A great Synod
Of all the parties
Has trampled down
Dogmas and ceremonies.

A number of Wergeland's writings express the idea that Christianity has deep roots in common with other religions. In "Napoleon", from his first collection of poems, *Digte. Første Ring* ("Poems. The First Ring"), which was published in 1829, he describes the one true God behind the different faiths:

> The Gods of old were spirits
> God sent to earth, in earthly garments dressed,
> So they might tread
> Reason's first footsteps.

Benterud writes: "His hope that Christianity would triumph over all other religions did not mean he despised the others but that he felt that Christianity contained the natural religion in its purest form. He believed that it would triumph through the idea of truth and freedom, not by violence or force".

Thus in Wergeland's view all religions are at heart expressions of the faith he himself had arrived at through his all-embracing love of nature and of all creation, which he believed originated in the one true God.

In his wonderful poem "My Little Rabbit", addressed to his pet Blaamin and written at almost the same time as *Creation, Man and Messiah*, Wergeland describes the relationship between the rabbit, the poet and God in terms of the same chain of life depicted in the longer poem:

> In my rabbit's eyeball clear
> Through the lens's rainbow veil
> Through the pupil's cylinder

Heaven's wide span on high I see
(God's this bosom broad and wide,
Wherein the mite dares warm itself
In the sun's rays)
Seething with life, from the gnat's spark
The mammoth's flames, to the sun's blaze ... my little pet
This panorama in your eye did lie.
...
(Behold the glance that I did cast
Into the Creator's fantasy!)
...
How great the vision I was granted!
Sight of life, sight of becoming!
As a lightening lit on high
Enflames mist's effervescing fire.
Soon a thousand others burn.
Water, air and colours arose,
Poles and courses, zones and goals
Around the millions of suns
...
Almighty God, lighting the sun,
Of mist myself and Blaamin made

This religious imagery is in line with the ideas of Christian Neoplatonism: life is the result of a never-ending radiation of divine light, an emanation from God himself, and takes form as links in a chain, which starts with the lowest forms of life and rises through higher and higher beings on the path back to their divine origin. The rabbit is at a lower level than the human being on this chain, but both are equally valuable parts of God's indivisible creation and are intimately linked with each other in that they each occupy their necessary place on an unbroken ladder leading back to God. Characteristically, this theological student and poet maintains in "My Little Rabbit" that he does not primarily derive his understanding of God and His Creation from reading the Bible. He approaches God through his poetic imagination, in this poem his "harp". He is aware of God's immanence in nature through the medium of his own creative imagination. But as I have pointed out above, there is no sharp boundary between Wergeland's imagination and his Romantically influenced notion of reason. He sees God more clearly in the eye of his rabbit than he would be able to do through any amount of reading:

Blaamin, when alone your friend
Glumly in his corner pored
O'er his ancient book deriving
From the Jewish temple old
...
[The poet]
Hurled it then so far away
That the book could not be found,
Fancying that his harp's spread wings
Would bear him through the firmament
To Heaven far more swiftly than
This musty tome, its pages filled
With rotted words
...

147

Then the source of life I saw,
In my corner, as a spring
Refreshing wells; its drops were falling
Clearer far than in my book!

This all-embracing idea of God is also reflected in the poem
"In the Thunder", published together with "My Little
Rabbit" in *Poems. First Ring.* Here the young Wergeland
writes of a furious storm, which with thunder and slashes of
lightening spreads death and terror over the earth:

Thunder rolling o'er the earth
Lighting up the Northern sky
Like a phosphorescent sea
...
Lightning's scarlet Midgard serpent,
Thunder's black and golden wolf
Beneath the rainbow's vaulted arch

The thunderclouds are "flags of death", and a battle rages
in the heavens while the earth buries itself in sorrow. All it
can do is remain wordless, groan and hope that in the end
life will prevail. Yet in the midst of this Armageddon mankind perceives that lightening, dread and darkness are also
expressions of a divine greatness:

Away with earthly, song-filled temples
And canting priests! I will worship my God
To the song of the heavens

...
A chorus of praise
With fiery tongues.

All the faithful can take part in worshipping the almighty God who reveals himself in the storm, and Wergeland allows them considerable room for expression. First the Jew Nathan:

Allah opens His heaven
...
The Prophet – behold the lightening! – draws his sword
To cleave his sacred path

Then comes the Muslim Ali:

Look, that same battle
Rages in your human breast:
A divine lightening in your heartbeat,
A black thunder in your loins and veins

The different expressions of faith cause the poet to ask:

Yet whose song with thunder ringing
Best his soul did praise his God!
May Christian, Muslim, Heathen, Jew
Ultimately meet each other
In their common Father's arms.

149

Each with his own melody
Sought to enter the same hall
And in the smoke of burning tears
Found comfort in each other's breast!

All dogmas are abandoned; the representatives of the various religions see one and the same God manifest himself through natural phenomena.

Wergeland's great poem "Caesaris" was not published until 1833, but he is thought to have written it in 1831. The content of the poem is so revolutionary that Wergeland's father, Nicolai, tried to persuade him not to publish it. When it finally did come out, the title had been changed; the original title, "Nicolai", was the name of the current Tsar of Russia, who in 1831 had brutally crushed the Polish insurrection. However, in spite of the new title the reference is obvious. The clear political message is underlined by Wergeland's religious belief, which here too forms a bridge between the different religions.

In the poem the Tsar's evil deeds have so oppressed the world that it seems as if God is no longer listening to people's prayers. But, says the poet, the Tsar is not ignored either in the Bible or in the Koran. The one true God, who manifests himself through both these sacred books, fulfils his word: "And God saw every thing that he had made, and … it was very good" and he grants salvation to the dying people. When this almighty God imposes thunder on the earth, he does so in order to prevent the Tsar from transforming the world into desert and chaos. The burning flames are the smiles of God's wisdom, the sparks from the fire are his eyes. Beyond the smoke and ashes lies a better future. The earth will again be green.

Thus even in his early years as a writer, Wergeland believed that the different world religions worshipped the same God. He preaches religious tolerance in many of his early poems and articles, and as his writing matured he continued to develop this theme. It also underlay his political activities, which were founded on compassion, human worth and human freedom. In the years from 1840 until his death in 1845, the mature poet put into practice what he had written in "Why does humanity progress so slowly?": Wergeland the theologian taught the common people in his educational booklets; he set aside all excluding dogmas and worked for political progress built on his belief in love, freedom and truth seen from the perspective of a universal God.

It was this world view that underlined Wergeland's efforts to get the Norwegian parliament to amend Article 2 of the Constitution, which prohibited Jews from entering Norway. He wrote an enormous number of poems and articles promoting what he considered to be both a human right and the will of God. Although this cause balked so large in Wergeland's life, there is only space in this article for an outline of the subject. However, some of these works are relevant here since they throw light on his religious views.

The collection of poems entitled *The Jew. Nine Blossoming Briar Shoots* was published in 1842. It contains the great poem "The Three", in which Wergeland says: *"Every religion has a mild and loving heart"*, written in italics. Partly in prose and partly in verse, the poem tells of three travellers who are crossing the Syrian desert:

a Jewish rabbi, a Christian monk and a Muslim mullah – Wergeland calls him a Mohammedan. The three men meet at an oasis, where they spend the night beneath the protective branches of a plane tree. They wake with the dawn: "The desert lay beneath the mist within its horizon like a vast violet-blue ocean encircled by mountains covered with the glorious roses of Damascus. At one point in the east angels seemed to be busy putting up golden spears as for a tent. The travellers could see that the sun was on the point of rising." Each of the men now longed to praise God in his own way, but did not like to do so because he was afraid of wounding the other two. "They were men with tact and feeling for each other and respect for the others' beliefs." But when three birds of three different species perched in the plane tree burst into song, the men are no longer able to keep silent, and each raises his voice in a song of praise to the One who created himself and all other things. In fact, says Wergeland, the songs are directed at one and the same God, even though the singers are addressing Him by different names:

"Allah, Allah, great and good!
Ever more be Allah praised!
See his word in floods of light
From his paradise out-flowing."
...
"To Jehovah praise and thanks!
Mercy are his sternest judgments.
See the cloud-hills, how they tremble!
Seraphs in the Orient soar..."
...

"Thanks and praise to God almighty!
See the morning light beginning—
To proclaim his name afar!"

But it is not enough to pronounce God's name. The monk's song of praise ends with the promise of the all-merciful love that shines over the earth and reveals:

… an Eden
Opened by the God of Mercy,
Round by rosy day-breaks girded,
In whose clouds
Saints among the crowds of angels
With unfettered tongues are praising
The Unnameable's high name.

Egil Wyller (quoted in Groven Myhren 2007) believes that "the Unnameable's high name" is the climax of the song of praise and thus constitutes a meeting place for the three religions. He views the last verses as an expression of religious mysticism, maintaining that "the meeting place of all three, indeed of all great religions, is contained in this paradox. A universal intellectual mysticism is revealed in which all names, all languages, all thoughts are brought to silence and stillness within the mystery of God – the Unnameable name."

"Thus it sounded simultaneously from the believers' breasts," writes Wergeland. "Thus it sounded simultaneously from the believers' breasts. They shook hands and now set out joyfully each in his direction through the desert: the Mollah journeyed toward Bagdad, the monk toward Jerusalem, the Rabbi toward Damascus." But each of them felt that with the help of the angels he had overcome his human frailty and was able to share with the others his song of praise to the one, common, highest God.

Thus "The Three" is more than just a poem about religious tolerance. In line with the main themes of Wergeland's work its message is based on his fundamental belief that the different human religions are culturally dependent expressions of faith in one and the same unnameable God.

This view is also expressed in a later work published in 1844, *The Jewess. Eleven Blossoming Briar Shoots.* In "The Women in the Churchyard" Wergeland describes how a meeting between three women among the graves causes them to put aside all hate and enmity, and enables them to join hands in the spirit of fellowship. There in the churchyard is "peace unbroken", it is "the forecourt of Heaven, where every man /– Sinner, saint, good or evil – / Casts his heaviest burden off, / His body formed of flesh and blood".

In this consecrated place, dedicated to peace, two women are walking arm in arm, one a Catholic and one a (Lutheran) Protestant. Catholic Rosalie's little daughter has just died, and she is looking for a beautiful site for her grave. Protestant Konstance draws her attention to burial plots both for Catholics and for herself, so that after death the two of them may "continue / In a sense to see each other". They then see a third woman, a Jewess, who is mourning a loved one beside a grave in the isolated corner of the churchyard that is the Jewish cemetery. Rosalie is displeased that in this area, which people have tried to fence off and separate from the rest of the churchyard, the plants have run wild in a way "that mocks law and order". Konstance agrees. She says that they do not wish to be associated with "this vile neighbourhood", and that the Jews must find another burial place. But the Jewess begins talking to them, and shows them an ornament she is wearing on her forehead, which is made up of a blue sapphire, a green emerald and a red ruby. She says that the "sapphire's light" is a symbol of the Catholic Church and the emerald of all the Protestant churches, while the ruby symbolises the pain and blood of the Jewish people. It is not possible, she says, to claim that one stone is worth more than any of the others. In the sun they all shine with an equal fire and have an equal significance that is independent of their colour:

See, oh see! How with the sun
Each through its colour radiates
An equal Heaven back again.
That is the value of each stone:
Its radiant power, not its hue,
Not blue nor green nor red reflection.

The Jewess goes on to explain her parable: the worth of each individual can only be measured in terms of the concept of God that has been planted in her heart and that she herself reflects back in the form of her deeds:

Only through the thought of God
And respect for God's command
Filling the soul, as does the sun

155

The jewels light,
Only that and that alone
Is proof by which a man's true worth
Can be tried and can be judged.

Such souls, wherever they may be,
Spread o'er the earth,
Together, bound by Heaven, will form
God's congregation, true, unseen.
And ever when its limbs do knock
Against each other, though they are
In caftan or in cowl attired,
They will on hearing "Peace!"
"Be tolerant!"
Know they have a member met
Of God's true congregation.

This poem also calls on everyone to practise religious tolerance, because they are all part of the same congregation and fundamentally share the same faith. Wergeland also expressed this message in his text for a sermon on "The Watchword of Christianity", published in 1845 as part of his series of educational booklets *For Arbeidsklassen* [For the Working Class]. Here he writes that those who live their lives in truth, hope and love have a stake in eternal salvation. He says that those who are not Christians can also attain salvation:

Of the three pillars of a Christian soul, it is truth and hope that are Christianity's characteristics, since love may be found in the breast of anyone of any faith; and since a love based on deeds is the only unconditional duty, incorporating in itself all duties, we dare not, unless out of blind eagerness we ourselves reject love, deny such people a firm place among the good in this world and among the saved in the next, where creeds will not divide and where faith will be converted into true awareness.

In February 1845, as Wergeland was dying, he received a prayer book as a gift from a pastor named Wilhelm Andreas Wexels. In a letter to his father, Wergeland wrote that he responded to the pastor's gift "by remarking that I believed I found more strength in the gaze I turned so painfully on the stars at night. In my funeral procession I would prefer to have an honest heathen and a faithful dog rather than Christians who, in the name of their Christianity, would refuse to walk behind my coffin." In this letter he does not distance himself from Christians as such, but from those who have isolated themselves in a separate faith and rejected Wergeland for not being a true believer. The heathen and the dog, he says, are closer to God than such people. Thus his reason for rejecting Wexels' attempt to influence him was that he found religious intolerance unacceptable; all creatures are equally close to God.

Benterud claims that Wergeland's indifference to the Church increased after 1840, when he became Director General of the National Archives. "He uses fewer ecclesiastical turns of phrase," she says. "But the person of Jesus never ceased to fascinate him." Nor did Wergeland ever renounce his faith in God. Throughout his adult life he retained the deep religious feeling acquired during his youth. Characteristically, when on his deathbed he strongly affirmed his faith in God, he made it clear that *his* God was the God of all people and all creation, and was not limited to any particular faith.

In one of his last letters to his father, dated 17 May 1845, less than a month before he died, he says that his "ideas about God's greatness and my own insignificance are of great comfort to me. I die a Deist, a sincere worshipper of Allah; out of respect I would not presume to conjecture in any detail what awaits me in the next world or how that world is ordered."

This does not of course mean that Wergeland died a Muslim, as a number of newspaper articles have rather naively suggested. As a theologian he is likely to have known that Arabic-speaking Jews and Christians also use the name Allah for God. For Wergeland the name of God was unimportant; he used the word to refer to the God who created and sustained the whole world and was the common God of all mankind. He believed that the mystery of God is not revealed in the names people have given him. As we see in "The Three", Wergeland called this God the "Unnameable".

Wergeland died believing in a personal, almighty God who created all things. Throughout his adult life he perceived God as immanent, present in the smallest creature and the highest being, in a feeble blade of grass and in the individual's longing for love and freedom. His life and writing are imbued with a religious belief that is not confined by any dogma, whether that of Judaism, of Islam or of Christianity – for Wergeland all human beings were equal in the sight of God. Nor did he see any difference between God and his creation. For him the whole world was permeated with divine truth, freedom and love, given as gifts to all mankind, and he believed that every individual had been made responsible for putting these values into practice in his earthly life. However, Wergeland's God is still always present, to create and sustain, and never quite abandons the individual or leaves him to rely on himself alone.

List of references

Benterud, Aagot [undated]. *Henrik Wergelands religiøse utvikling: en litteraturhistorisk studie* [Henrik Wergeland's Religious Development, from the Point of View of Literary History]. Oslo, Dreyers forlag.

Groven Myhren, Dagne 2007. "'Smukke Skyer' – Henrik Wergelands sognekall". In Johansen, Ronnie et al (eds.) *Ble Henrik Wergeland muslim? – en debattbok,* pp. 63–70 ["'Beautiful Clouds' – Henrik Wergeland's call to the priesthood", in "Did Henrik Wergeland Become a Muslim?"].

Johanson, Ronnie and Kjartan Selnes 2007. *Ble Henrik Wergeland muslim?: en debattbok.* [A Debate on 'Did Henrik Wergeland Become a Muslim?'] Oslo, Norwegian Humanist Association.

Wergeland, Henrik 1918-40. *Samlede Skrifter* [Collected Works, 23 vols, critical edition]. Jæger, Herman, Didrik Arup Seip, Halvdan Koht and Einar Høigård (eds). Kristiania/Oslo.

HENRIK WERGELAND

The three

Translated from the Norwegian by Illit Grøndahl

What wonderful temples of human charity are not the public hostels of the Orientals! Turks and Bukhars have their caravan-serails, the Persians their khans, the Hindus their temple-like resting places, the Beduins and the wild Kabyles their inviolable marabouts, and everyone without distinction is at home in the Arab's tent. Had he been a richer man, and had he not lived scattered over the desert, he also would have built caravan-serails and khans for the stranger, for those are nothing but an exalted transform-ation of the tent of his fathers. It is the same hospitability of the tent which has opened those spacious stone-built halls in which the travelling Turk binds his steed and feels well at ease, where the Armenian takes in his camel, where the Jew or the Nazarene finds room for his bundle and himself in the ever open hospitable cells.

Every religion has a mild and loving heart. These bene-volent institutions are due to the one which we Christians believe to have the hardest heart. They are religious in their origins, whether they have been created at public or private cost. The latter is often the case. The pious Mohammedan or Hindu bequeaths to these hostels as the Christian does to

161

churches, convents and hospitals. It is *the whole* of human-kind that he in his heart wishes to help when he builds such a hostel with gates open to the four corners of the world, or sinks a well in the desert, or leads a fresh fountain to the resting-place of the beasts. Also of them does he think the old, grim, bearded philanthropist whom Allah, Brahma, and the God of the Christians bless!

Somewhere beyond the Dead Sea there is in sunscorched Syria a desert, which the infidels' charity has gone by—, not that it not has been discovered, but because Allah just at the journey's end has here given a natural caravan-serail in the shape of a gigantic plane-tree with room, shelter and fresh water for a whole caravan if needed. Chance brought together here one evening a Mohammedan, a Christian, and a Jew. The Mohammedan, a mollah or priest, had scarcely watered his horse, before a black spot on the horizon fore-told a stranger's arrival. This was the Christian, a monk of the Order of the Holy Mount. A mule carried him from Haleb to Jerusalem. "Salem aleikum!" said the Mollah to the Nazarene, who returned his greeting in God's name. The stars were already glittering and the howl of the jackals was heard when the Jew, a rabbi from Damascus, unno-ticed—for he came on foot—stepped on to the small plot of grass which the fountain had called forth under the plane-tree. In the days of King Solomon the fountain had also fostered this tree, and the latter had now in return as a good foster-son supported his foster-mother with his shade. Like mothers in their old age the motherly spring was still singing her lullaby. By this murmur the three travellers after friendly converse at last fell asleep, each in his root-hollow of the gigantic tree, and by the same murmur they woke up in the early dawn.

The desert lay beneath the mist within its horizon like a vast violet-blue ocean encircled by mountains covered with the glorious roses of Damascus. At one point in the east angels seemed to be busy putting up golden spears as for a tent. The travellers could see that the sun was on the point of rising. Something moved their hearts, their lips trembled. Each one of them wished to greet God in his way, but alas!—each was afraid of wounding the feelings of the other two. In the course of their talk on the previous evening they had learned to respect each other; but now,—how could the Mollah worship Allah aloud without disturbing the devotions of the Nazarene and the Jew, and likewise with the others. And still the need to give vent to their hearts' feeling in this supreme moment, and to thank the Highest for his protection in the paradisaic shelter they had enjoyed, was so great in each of them that their lips trembled. None, however, yet broke the silence. Quietly and hesitatingly the Mohammedan strapped the saddle on his horse without getting done with it. The monk showed no more expedition with his mule, the Rabbi tied and tied his bundle. They were men with tact and feeling for each other and respect for the others' belief. Already thousands of glittering lances gleamed over the top of the rose-mountain. In the next moment the glorious image of the most High would appear, and the worshippers should remain silent? The lips of all three trembled; but no prayer, no hymn of praise sounded from them.

Then,—at the same moment, from the same branch of the plane-tree a bullfinch, a wagtail and a thrush begin their morning song. The clear trill of the bullfinch blended with the warbling of the other birds in a glorious, jubilant choir.

"Why do we tarry, brethren?" they all exclaimed. "Yes, with that which is on our lips?" said the Mollah, bending three times to the earth. "With the praise of Jehovah, the Highest?" said the Rabbi, folding his hands across his breast. "Yes," said the Christian priest, making the sign of the cross,— "is this not a sign from Heaven that our praise also will be pleasing to the Lord, although our expression of it be different?" And of a sudden, like the birds overhead, they all three with a kindly glance to each other, each in his way, burst out in a song of praise to the Creator of them and of all things.

The Mollah sang:
"Allah, Allah, great and good!
Evermore be Allah praisèd!
See his word in floods of light
From his paradise out-flowing.
See the Prophet's great commandment:
"Worship Allah, love thy neighbour!"
Over all the heavens scattered,
In the beams reflected, gently
Touching every tiny leaflet.

Ah, the distant palm is glowing
Like a Kaaba's vaulted dome!
E'en the grass
Turns toward the East adoring;

164

And the fig-leaf's stainless hands,
Bathed in dewy baptism,
Lift themselves as if they would
Blend their humble, silent prayers
With Life's sounding shouts of joy:
Allah, Allah, evermore
Praise and glory without ending
Be to Him who for the worm seeks
Underneath the fern's cold frondage
With the mild warmth of His goodness,
For its need to satisfy,—
He who stretches
O'er the head of Earth's proud master
And o'er moment-living dust-mote
Love's enfolding, radiant arms—
Allah, Allah, thanks and praise!"

The Rabbi sang:
"To Jehovah praise and thanks!
Mercy are his sternest judgments.
See the cloud-hills, how they tremble!
Seraphs in the Orient soar…
See how all their wings are spreading.
Nearer, nearer they are coming
With loud cries of Hallelujah.

Gates of Eden wide are opened.
Cherubs wait to catch the sigh
That from Israel is rising.
Dire lament they glorify
To a choir of jubilation

Which they bear in
Triumph to the ear of Grace,
Showing to the sorrow-stricken
Victory's palms
O'er the throne of Peace extended.

Hallelujah! In the East
Mercy's rosary is broken:
All its beads, as rosebuds fair,
Cherub o'er the hills are flinging.
Yonder is a Zion rising
Radiant in the heavens' blue.
Solomonic temple towers
Golden-columned on its summit.
...See how glows with velvet purple
The interior!
Golden red
Seven-armed candelabrum
Like a constellation shines
From a gloom of deepening scarlet,
When it breaks the waves of darkness.
Heaven above
Full of David's harps is hung.
Clangor of the stricken gold
From the morning cloud is bursting.
And on either side extended
Are along th' horizon's brow
Tents of the twelve tribes serenely
In the sunrise Canaan.[26]

---

[26] *Translator's note:* A liberty has here been taken in omitting the individual names
of the tribes.

Dawn is in Jehovah's judgments;
And their night will soon be over.
To the faithful
Shall Messiah yet be coming
Radiant from the heavens down."

And the Christian, the Nazarene, sang:
"Thanks and praise to God almighty!
See the morning light beginning—
To proclaim his name afar!
See the grass in tufted clusters
Bending down to Him who burdens
Also it with freshening dew.
For its holy water pure,
Sprinkled over grass and branches,
Sanctifies both grove and meadow
As a holy temple-hanging,
Of the mountain makes an altar,
Where the shining ones adore.

Every stem that sunlit glistens,
Falls and rises o'er the plain,
Is a leaning-staff of Faith;
Every leaf a wingéd angel,
every twig a cross of gold,
Wherewith all the air is swarming.
Every flower the sun has gilded
Is a cup by mercy filled.
Heavenly love has tenderly
All its heart poured out into it,
Reached the chalice, overflowing,

To each guileless being, open
To the e'er-renewed ascension
Daily from the morning clouds,—
To the promise that is written
On the dew-besilvered meadow
Of a Love all-merciful,
Beaming forth in mildest radiance,
Flowing from the fullest cups
On our parched and darksome Earth,
Of an Eden
Opened by the God of Mercy,
Round by rosy day-breaks girded,
In whose clouds
Saints among the crowds of angels
With unfettered tongues are praising
The Unnameable's high name."

Thus it sounded simultaneously from the believers' breasts. They shook hands and now set out joyfully each in his direction through the desert: the Mollah journeyed toward Bagdad, the monk toward Jerusalem, the Rabbi toward Damascus. But when they had got a little distance into the desert, it was as though the same thought stopped them and made them send a grateful glance back to the hospitable plane-tree, which now lay far away like a St. Helena in the ocean of air.

Illit Grøndahl's translation of "The Three" was first published in Henrik Wergeland. Poems, *Gyldendal Norsk Forlag, Oslo 1929.*

CONTRIBUTORS

Geir Pollen (b. 1953) is a recognised Norwegian writer of fiction, who published his first work in 1982. His long list of titles includes both novels and poetry, a number of which have been translated into several languages.

Iver Neumann (b. 1959) is Professor in Russian Studies at the University of Oslo and Research Professor at the Norwegian Institute of International Affairs.

Mette Lending (b. 1972) is a historian. She has worked for several years as a consultant to the Ministry of Foreign Affairs on cultural exchange issues.

Vigdis Ystad (b. 1942) is Professor of Nordic Literature at the University of Oslo, and editor-in-chief of the new critical edition of Henrik Ibsen's writings.